404 Terrific
TECH TIPS

The Best of AMERICAN WOODWORKER™ magazine

A RODALE PRESS PUBLICATION

CONTENTS

AMERICAN WOODWORKER, the premiere magazine for the woodworking enthusiast, is published by Rodale Press, Inc., 33 E. Minor Street, Emmaus, PA 18098. To subscribe, please call 1-800-666-3111.

CONTENTS

INTRODUCTION

Everybody likes a good idea and here are 404 great ones. This valuable collection will entertain you and inspire you, and you're sure to find a dozen valuable ideas you can put right to work in your own workshop.

This collection of shop tips comes from the Tech Tips column in AMERICAN WOODWORKER magazine. This column is the magazine's most popular feature, and no wonder, for these workshop ideas and devices come straight from the practical experience of America's woodworkers. This is shop-tested advice guaranteed to help you work better and smarter. You'll have more fun woodworking, and who knows, perhaps you'll be inspired to share your own best ideas.

David Sloan
Editor & Publisher

Shop, Bench and Vise

Wedge Vise

This simple holding device is best suited for gripping a board (or door or similar assembly) by its edge. It can be installed on a plank, sawhorse or on the workbench. I make mine out of 2x8 stock, but yours should suit the work you do. I use a wedge angle of about 15 deg. and a bevel angle on the wedge of about 35 deg. A tap on the wedge secures or releases the workpiece.

John Hagen
East Jordan, MI

Improvised Hold-downs

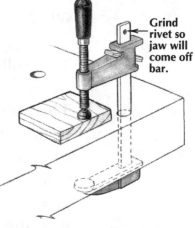

Four-inch Jorgensen bar clamps make excellent bench hold-downs. All you need do is grind off the rivet so the sliding jaw can be slipped off the bar. Then drill holes in the bench at convenient intervals, push the bar through one of the holes, and reinstall the sliding jaw. You can put the handle above or below the bench— whichever is more convenient.

Grind rivet so jaw will come off bar.

D.E. Brumfield
Lesage, WV

Bench Stop

If your workbench lacks bench dogs and a tail vise, this simple plywood bench stop will hold stock firmly for planing or belt sanding.

Cut the jig from 3/4-in. plywood and screw it to the left front corner of your bench (right front corner if you're left-handed). Tap in the wedge to clamp the stock.

Bill Bigelow
Surry, NH

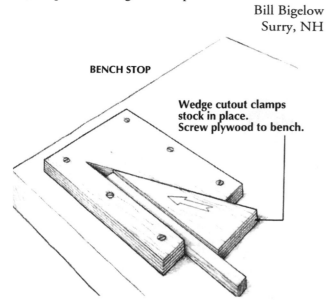

BENCH STOP

Wedge cutout clamps stock in place. Screw plywood to bench.

Bench Mounted C Clamp

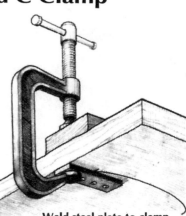

I use a fixed C clamp mounted to my work table to hold parts in jigs and fixtures. It takes the place of expensive toggle clamps and is easy to use one-handed.

I weld a lx5-in. length of 1/4-in. thick steel plate on the fixed end of the clamp. I usually locate the centerline of the plate on the centerline of the clamp. I pre-drill and countersink the plate for three or four #12 flat head screws, which fasten the plate to the underside of the table.

A 5-in. or 6-in. C clamp such as Jorgenson #175 or #176 offers plenty of throat depth. A battery of these clamps along one edge of the bench, is great for laminating.

Weld steel plate to clamp.

Patrick Warner
Escondido, CA

New Uses for Corner Molding

I've found that sections of 3/4-in. wood corner molding are ideal for padding the jaws of a metal vise. Self-adhesive magnetic strips keep them in place. When they get chewed up, it takes only a minute to replace them.

The same molding, with the corner up, makes a stand when using several long-handled artist's brushes.

Craig Bentzley
Chalfont, PA

Benchtop Extension

When I needed to plane some extra-long stock, I improvised a 2 ft. extension for my benchtop as shown. It projects far enough that I can clamp the work between the stop on the end of the extension and the dog in the tail vise at the other end of the bench. I've also made some shorter extensions by nailing a plywood "L" to a scrap piece of 2x4.

Carl Dorsch
Pittsburgh, PA

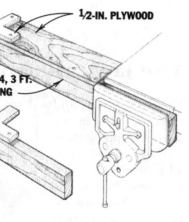

Slipnot Slips Not

I recently found the ideal material to stop work from sliding around on the bench. It's called "Slipnot" and is used in mobile homes to keep things in place when on the road. The advantage of Slipnot is that it's waterproof so you can just rinse it under a faucet (or give it a good shaking) when it gets dusty or full of wood chips. It comes in 12-in. wide rolls, sells for about $1 a foot and is available in camping supply stores.

Douglas Mertz
Meredith, NH

Magnetic Vise Blocks

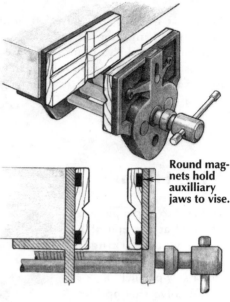

I devised these special jaws for holding dowels or turned work in a regular wood vise. I made the auxiliary jaws on the tablesaw by cutting two shallow, bisecting "V"s in two scrap blocks. Then, instead of screws I used small round magnets to attach the blocks to the vise. This way I can quickly remove the auxiliary jaws and also rotate them to any convenient angle. I have a second set, with no V's, that I use for my regular work.

Dick Dorn
Oelwein, IA

Quick Change Vises

I had no room to mount a machinist's vise on my workbench, so I mounted the vise on a T-shaped wooden base. When I need the vise, I clamp the base in the jaws of my woodworking vise.

Clarence H. Fraley
Loyall, KY

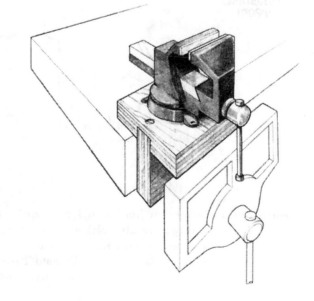

Skateboard Helper

Now that my two sons have left home I don't have their help around my shop anymore. But they left behind their skateboards, and I've found these useful for moving heavy objects like 3/4-in. plywood. I just stand the edge of a sheet on a skateboard and move it with the greatest of ease.

Bobby L Martin
Marion, SC

Vise Helper

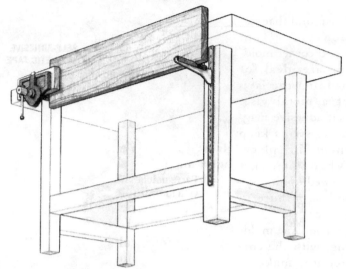

It's hard to grip a piece of wood at one end of many woodworking vises because the jaws don't stay parallel.

To solve this problem, drop a block the same thickness as the stock you want to grip in the other end of the vise. The vise jaws will stay parallel, and you'll get a better grip. Nails will keep the block from slipping through the vise jaws and dropping on the floor.

William Guthrie
Pontiac, MI

Multi-Purpose Bench

I use this low bench in a number of ways: as an assembly table; for sanding and routing; and for cutting plywood with a Skilsaw. I also find it useful to support cabinets or

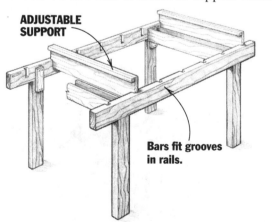

ADJUSTABLE SUPPORT

Bars fit grooves in rails.

other projects at a convenient height so I can work on them. Since the fastenings are all bolts and sheetrock screws, the bench comes apart for moving or storage.

Donald Taylor
Deer River, MI

Long-Board Support

Woodworkers have contrived a great many devices to hold up the end of a long board clamped in a vise, but few are as simple and reliable as this one. Screw an ordinary metal shelf standard to a leg of the workbench. Fit it with a shelf bracket and a piece of split tubing or hose for cushioning.

John McDonald
Englishtown, NJ

Vise Jaw Cushions

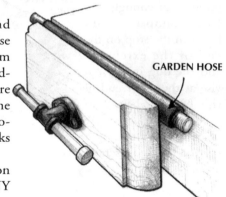

GARDEN HOSE

I protect dowels and threaded rod from vise jaws by Slipping them into a piece of discarded garden hose before clamping them in the vise. Rubber automotive heater hose works for larger diameters.

W. J. Morrison
Northport, NY

Stop Pinching Handles

If you have iron handles in your face vise you know that they're not just noisy; they can also give your finger a nasty pinch. Just slip a rubber O-ring over each end of the handle and you've tamed it for good. Wooden handles also are improved by a couple of O-rings: The end caps lose their maddening habit of popping off and dropping the handle.

Andy Rae
Lenhartsville, PA

Workmate Machine Bench

Those of us with limited shop space can't afford the luxury of floor-mounted machines. I attach my benchtop jointer, shaper, 10-in. Ryobi planer, etc., to sturdy wood mounting plates so they can still be stored compactly. When needed, I lift the machine onto my Black & Decker Workmate, clamp it, and it's ready for business.

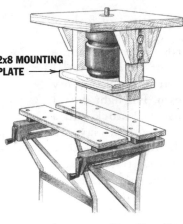

2x8 MOUNTING PLATE

Ron Pavelka
Orange, CA

Woodworker's Bench Hook and Holding Jig

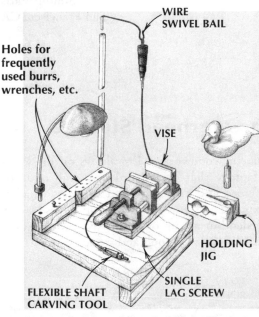

Holes for frequently used burrs, wrenches, etc.

WIRE SWIVEL BAIL

VISE

HOLDING JIG

SINGLE LAG SCREW

FLEXIBLE SHAFT CARVING TOOL

This is an ideal bench hook for small carvings and can be made from scrap 2x12. I mount the model-maker's vise on a short piece of 1x4 and then lag-screw it to the bench hook. By slackening the bolt I can rotate the vise to any convenient position.

I made the carver's holding jig from a piece of 2x3, slotted and drilled for a 5/8-in. dowel as shown. To hold my work securely, I cut the head off a 2-in. drywall screw and epoxied the shank into the end of the dowel.

Chuck Malvern
Bremerton, WA

Extension Dogs

My Workmate bench still serves me well but is too narrow for some jobs. To solve this problem, I made four 8-in. extenders with dowels that fit in the predrilled holes in the bench platform. With these extension dogs in place, I can hold panels up to twice the width of the bench.

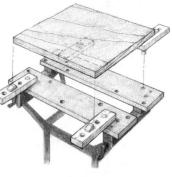

Robert Graul
Alton, IL

Double-Duty Dog Holes

If you build (or convert) your workbench with dog holes large enough to accommodate a 3/4-in. pipe, you can conveniently clamp awkward shapes directly to your benchtop. You can then assemble a pipe clamp right through the benchtop.

Glenn Hughes
Dublin, PA

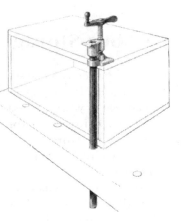

Portable Bench Light

I needed a light I could place anywhere on my bench. To do this, I drilled a 1/2-in. hole in the top of a wooden bench dog to fit a flexible-arm lamp. Get the lamp before you drill to be sure that you make the right sized hole.

Yeung Chan
Millbrae, CA

Overhead Storage

I devised this rack to keep my supply of dowels organized and visible, yet out of the way. I clamped three pieces of plywood together and drilled holes with a 2 1/8-in. hole saw. My rack has each dowel size clearly marked and accommodates lengths from 18 in. to 4 ft.

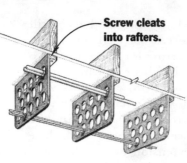

Screw cleats into rafters.

Craig Bentzley
Chalfont, PA

Lumber-Storage Brackets

Storing lumber is always a problem. I made wall brackets a couple of years ago and have been using them for heavy lumber storage ever since. They're inexpensive and easy to make.

I bolted the brackets to the wall studs with 1/4 x 2 1/4-in. lag bolts and washers. I installed the brackets on 32-in. centers. For light loads, 48-in. centers will do.

J.P. Reichling
Oswego, IL

Expanding Upwards

When a crowded city runs out of room it expands upwards. I apply the same logic when storing clamps in my basement shop. I clamp hand screws directly to the overhead joists and fasten C-clamps to a board screwed to the bottom edge of a joist. Spring clamps are best clipped onto a thin board screwed to the side of a joist.

Carl Dorsch
Pittsburgh, PA

Shop-Made Brackets

I got tired of forking out $2 or $3 every time I needed some shelf brackets, so I started making my own. For light duty I use 1x2 stock and a low angle, say 30 degrees. With more substantial loads, I might go to 45 deg. or even 60 deg. and use 2x4 stock. Reinforce the lipped box joint shown in the sketch with a couple of drywall screws.

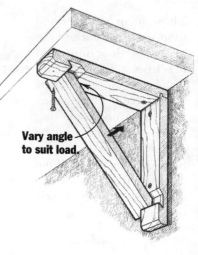

Vary angle to suit load.

To install, screw the bracket to the wall and then slide in the brace. There's no need for glue—gravity and friction keep it in place. I've used these brackets for shelves, lumber racks, to hang plants, and to support a bench grinder and a small drill press.

Simon Watts
San Francisco, CA

More on Overhead Storage

Like many amateur woodworkers I'm always on the lookout for extra storage that doesn't take up wall or floor space. So I designed and made plywood "drawers" that fit between the exposed joists in my workshop. These swing down when needed but are up out of my way when not. I fill my overhead drawers with tools and workshop items.

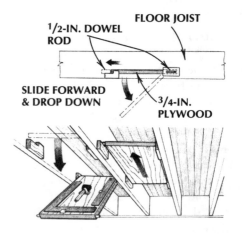

1/2-IN. DOWEL ROD

FLOOR JOIST

SLIDE FORWARD & DROP DOWN

3/4-IN. PLYWOOD

Kevin Bentley
Birmingham, MI

Sliding Storage

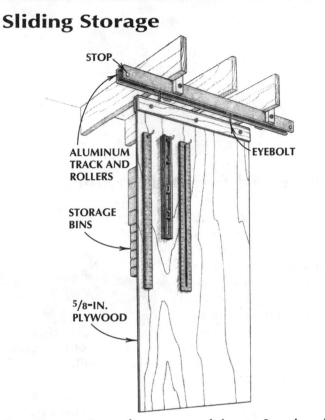

Space is scarce in my basement workshop so I made a sliding storage wall. One side has 11 rows of storage bins; on the other side I hang my straight edges, clamps, rulers and level. The unit is 3 ft. by 8 ft., but only 4½ in. in depth.

Bill Davis
Orange, CA

New Slant on an Old Racquet

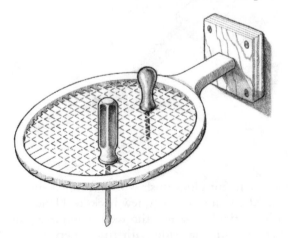

Here's how to use an old racquet—tennis, squash or badminton—in the shop. Just saw the handle off short and epoxy it into a piece of scrap. Screw this to a convenient spot on the wall and you're set. It's especially handy for small tools with handles such as awls and screwdrivers.

Robert Whiteside
Emporia, VA

Safe Shelf for Saws and Routers

A slotted shelf allows tools such as circular saws, saber saws and routers to be shelved in their natural position without damaging blades and bits.

Eleanor Hubbard
Knoxville, MD

Hang It Up

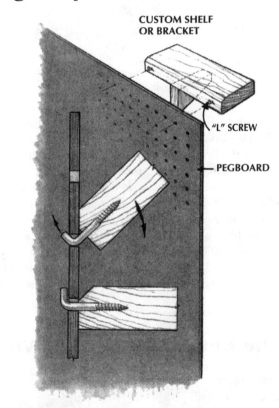

Do you have a drawer full of unused pegboard hooks and a workbench full of stuff that won't hang on the hooks? You can make your own shelves or custom-fitted hangers out of wood, and hang them on the peg-board using store-bought "L" screws on the back edge. Three things to watch: 1. "L" screw fits the pegboard; 2. horizontal spacing of the screws is exactly the same as the spacing of the holes; 3. top half of the back edge of your hang-up is chamfered.

Myron S. Levy
Gold Hill, OR

Tool Tactics

Plane from a Chisel

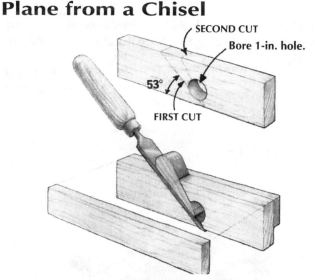

SECOND CUT
Bore 1-in. hole.
53°
FIRST CUT

To make a rabbet or plough plane from a chisel, select a piece of stable wood 2 or 3-in. wide by 8 or 9-in. long, and plane it to a thickness equal to the width of the chisel. Bore a 1-in. hole through it, just forward of the center and 1/4 in. or so from one edge. Next, cut it apart to give a cutting angle of about 53 degrees, and cut back the rear of the front section to make room for a wedge. Finally, glue on two side strips to hold the two pieces together. Make a wooden wedge to hold the chisel in position.

Ric Hanisch
Quakertown, PA

All the Better to See You With...

Attach magnifier with tape, wire or small hose clamps.

I recently found a new use for those flexible desk lamps in vogue years ago. After removing the bulb holder and wiring, I attached a large magnifying glass as shown. Now I can have both hands free when working on miniature projects.

Howard Moody
Upper Jay, NY

New Road for Old Drivers

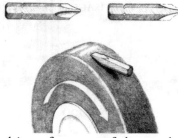

I use lots of Sheetrock screws, which are made of hardened steel. Even quality Phillips drivers soon start to skid and I have no way to sharpen them. Instead, I regrind them to fit a particular size of slotted screw, and I now have drivers for most of the regular sizes. All it takes is a bench grinder, a steady hand and about five minutes.

Simon Watts
San Francisco, CA

Low-tech Trim Saw

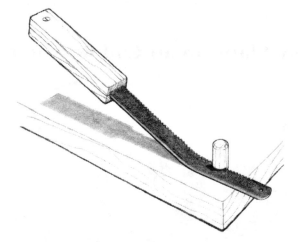

I have a way to cut plugs flush with a finished surface that doesn't need a router. I take a new hacksaw blade—the flat type with no ripples—grind the teeth completely off one side, then smooth that side with fine emery paper. The blade is flexible enough to be readily sprung down flat on a finished surface, and it won't leave any scratches.

You can make the blade cut on the push stroke or the pull—whichever you prefer—by attaching the wooden handle at one end or the other.

Paul Payne
Vero Beach, FL

Nail Holder

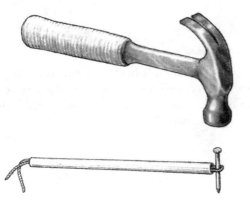

If your fingers can't reach to hold a nail where you need to start it, hold the nail with a loop of string through a soda straw. Slip the nail through the loop and pull the string tight to hold the nail.

Alice & Robert Tupper
Canton, SD

Three-Claw Retriever

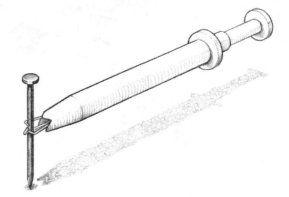

I was helping my dad make a picture frame and found it difficult to hold such small nails while driving them with a hammer. So I tried holding the nails with a three-claw part retriever, like the ones sold at computer supply stores. It was the perfect tool.

Matthew McDougal
Findlay, OH

Velcro Tape Holder

The spring clip that comes with most steel tapes often takes two hands to get back on the belt. I found this awkward, so I removed the spring clip altogether and epoxied a square piece of Velcro to the tape measure. Then I made a matching Velcro patch that I looped around my belt and stapled together. This tape holder is a great improvement.

Wesley Phillips
Greer, SC

Nail-Pulling Wedge

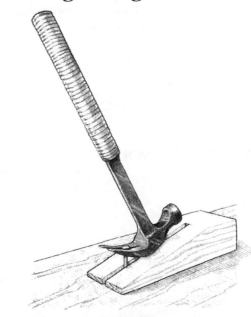

This wedge is useful when puffing nails—especially large ones. Slide the wedge forward as you extract the nail so the fulcrum stays close to the head. It works equally well with a wrecking bar.

Robert Tupper
Canton, SD

No-Split Nails

To prevent a nail from splitting the wood, put the head of the nail on a hard surface and blunt the point of the nail with your hammer. This will greatly reduce the chance of splitting the wood—especially hardwood.

Alvin H. Sherwood
Round Lake, IL

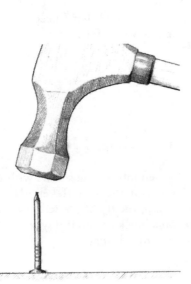

Handy Wax

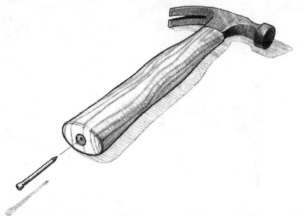

A finish nail goes into hard wood much more easily, and is less likely to curl up and die, if it is waxed first. I drill a hole in the end of my hammer handle and fill it with melted candle wax or paraffin to keep it handy. You couldn't find a better place to keep the wax.

Bradley Hankins
Arlington, TX

Cutting Wood Threads

When cutting wood threads with a thread box, try first soaking the stock to be threaded in linseed oil for 10 to 15 minutes. It makes for a cleaner cut and reduces moisture absorption that can cause the thread to jam.

Robert Maclaren
Harpster, OH

Slippery Screws

An old-time trick to make wood screws drive easier is to rub the screw over a cake of soap before driving.

Walter Morrison
Northport, NY

Extending Your Reach

For setting finish nails in those hard-to-reach places, I use a 3/8-in. ratchet drive extension over the nail set. It fits perfectly over the nail set, and light hammering does no damage to the extension.

Robert Welburn
Lake Worth, FL

Cheap Source for Beeswax

The beeswax you find in a toilet-bowl seal is excellent as a lubricant in the shop. Sold in hardware stores, toilet-bowl seals come in the shape of a large doughnut, so when I buy one I warm it, then re-form it in a tin can or small wooden box for storage. Beeswax is especially useful for lubricating screws, because it doesn't stain the wood.

Robert Behm
New Wilmington, PA

Tack Extractor

I needed a tool to remove tacks embedded in old lumber, so I took a worn-out jointer blade and ground one end to a round. Then I wrapped the other end with twine to make a handle. This little tool works so well that I keep finding new uses for it.

Louis Lopez
Plano, TX

Waxing Hot

When lubricating screws with paraffin wax I've noticed that most of the wax flakes off—especially in cold weather. Warm the tip of the screw with a match or lighter and lay it on a block of paraffin wax. This leaves a thin film of wax on the threads that stays put.

Alvin Cles
Boise, ID

A Quick Small Chisel

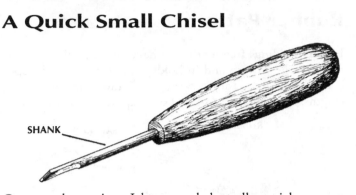

SHANK

On several occasions I have needed small special purpose chisels for inlaying or other small jobs. Rather than regrinding a regular chisel to do the job, I have been able to make some very good tools from small twist drills. You can make the handle from a short segment of 3/4-in. diameter dowels, shaped for a comfortable feel. Choose a twist drill of sufficient diameter. for example, I needed a chisel 1/28-in. wide and had a surplus of long shank 1/8-in. high-speed steel twist drills. I simply drilled a hole in the handle with one of these bits, deep enough to cover the twist, and used epoxy glue to anchor the twist end of the bit into the handle. The twist drill shank can now be ground to any shape or width desired. The cutting edge can be sharpened like any other chisel and these tools seem to hold a good edge.

Frank Pittman

Board Stretcher

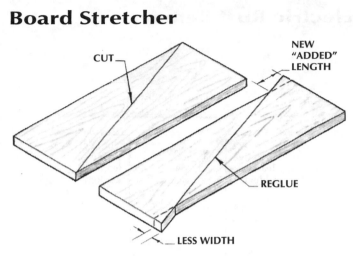

CUT

NEW "ADDED" LENGTH

REGLUE

LESS WIDTH

The next best idea to a board stretcher. It is possible to make boards longer if you have ample width. Cut the board diagonally, join and re-glue to desired length.

Christian Becksvoort

Low-Impact Glazing Points

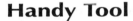

When driving glazing points in place with a hammer, place a steel or lead block against the muntin to absorb the shock. Wrap the block in paper to avoid scratching the glass.

Bill Bigelow
Surry, NH

Handy Tool

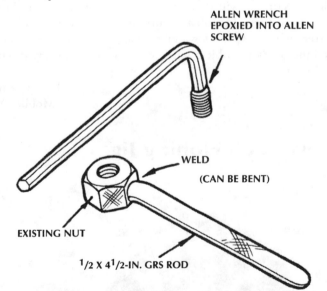

ALLEN WRENCH EPOXIED INTO ALLEN SCREW

WELD
(CAN BE BENT)

EXISTING NUT

1/2 X 4 1/2-IN. GRS ROD

I have a power tool with a table that had an underside nut which required adjusting for different operations, each time necessitating using a wrench. Welding a rod to the nut which needed frequent adjustment made the task so much easier. No longer did I need to search for the right wrench. Tighten the nut and mark to locate the handle.

Jay Wallace
Ashland, OR

Electric Rust Remover

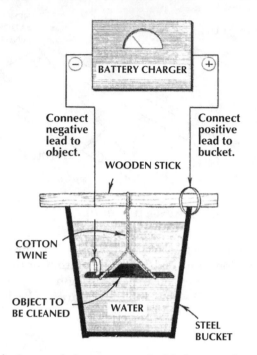

This device can bring unrecognizable lumps of rust back to useful forms. Here's how it works: You suspend the object to be cleaned in a steel bucket of water, then hook the negative lead from a battery charger to the object and the positive lead to the bucket. When you plug in the charger the electric current will draw off the rust. I usually wait about 10 hours, then shut off the current and retrieve the object. After using soap and water to wash off the greasy black residue, I dry the object with an old towel and spray it with WD-40.

David Leard
Mobile, AL

Low-Tech Honing Jig

I made this simple jig to hone plane irons while maintaining a constant angle. For chisels, or plane irons with no slot, I screw two drywall screws into the jig to hold the blade fast, one on each side of the blade.

Howard Ires
Danbury, CT

Rubber Pattern

I carve moldings frequently and have devised a jig to aid in marking the pattern and in holding the work. This is especially convenient for working small moldings and short lengths. First obtain a 1x4 or 1x6 scrap board which is flat.

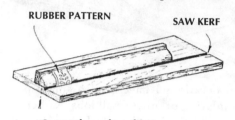

Cut a saw kerf the length of it about one third of the way in from the edge. The kerf will act as a guide for the pattern. The pattern is cut from rubber gasket material 1/8-in. thick. These dimensions are not critical but the rubber should slide along the kerf. Next screw from the back into the molding which has been placed along the kerf as shown. Leave the molding screwed to the board which, because it is wider and/or longer, is easily clamped to the bench, leaving the molding clear of annoying clamps and making the carving more efficient.

Frederick Wilbur
Lovingston, VA

Orbital Honing

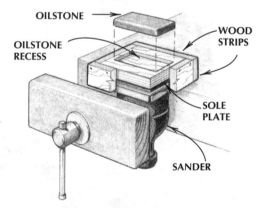

During my 50 years of woodworking I've found a simple, easy method to hone edges that you won't find in any textbook. First, I make a plywood plate to fit snugly over the pad of my orbital palm sander and cut a recess in the plywood to fit a small oilstone. Then I clamp the sander upside down in a vise with padded jaws, put in a stone and turn the sander on. The sander helps move the tool around so the stone wears evenly, and it's amazing how quickly and uniformly it hones a surface.

Milton Tucker
Salina, KS

Filing Bandsaw Blades

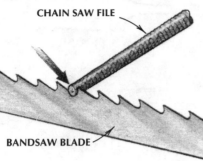

CHAIN SAW FILE

BANDSAW BLADE

One day I was caught with a job to finish, a dull bandsaw blade, and 30 miles to the nearest store. So I clamped the blade between two 12-in. pieces of 1x1-in. aluminum angle and went to work with a chain saw file. I filed straight across and found that two strokes would create a hook and sharpen the tooth. When I tried it out, the blade still had plenty of set and worked better than new.

Perry Samrow
Slidell, LA

Bevel-Angle Template

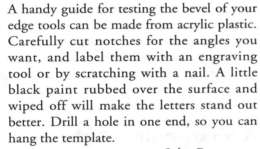

A handy guide for testing the bevel of your edge tools can be made from acrylic plastic. Carefully cut notches for the angles you want, and label them with an engraving tool or by scratching with a nail. A little black paint rubbed over the surface and wiped off will make the letters stand out better. Drill a hole in one end, so you can hang the template.

John Roccanova
Ancramdale, NY

Burnisher From Wrist Pin

Wrist pins from auto engines make ideal burnishers for putting a burr on hand scrapers and cabinet scrapers. They're very hard and can be highly polished. You can find wrist pins at junk yards and engine repair shops. They come in a variety of sizes. Look for hollow wrist pins so you can add a pair of handles.

H. Wesley Phillips
Greer, SC

Grinding Planer Blades

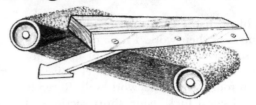

Here's a simple jig for sharpening planer and jointer blades on the belt sander. Move the block and blade back and forth across the sanding belt, concentrating pressure on the blade.

A.J. Tryba
Benton, IL

Drill Press Buffing Wheel

Instead of dedicating one side of a bench grinder to a buffing wheel we prefer to chuck the buffing wheel in a drill press. We find it's set at a more convenient working height and we like being able to control the speed (850 rpm or less works well with a 6 in. sewn muslin wheel). Also, we can keep the buffing wheel in a drawer when it's not in use.

When polishing the edge of a cutting tool be sure to work with the wheel's motion—not against it. Otherwise, the tool is likely to get caught by the spinning cloth and harpoon you.

Carolyn and John Grew-Sheridan
San Francisco, CA

Watering Japanese Stones

Japanese water stones are much more quickly saturated with water if, rather than completely submerging the stone, it is immersed up to, but not covering, the top surface. The air trapped in the stone escapes much more readily if its flow is not impeded by the in-rushing water. The plastic squeeze bottles in which contact lens solutions are packaged make excellent dispensers for water (or oil) when sharpening if they are carefully rinsed out beforehand.

Jesse D. Medlen
Plano, Tx

Carving Knives

Luthiers often use custom-made long-handle carving knives in their work. I have made a number of these knives using a variety of metals for the blades. Old high speed steel jointer knives or high carbon tool steel blanks work well. Recently we have had good luck using short sections of broken power hacksaw blades as the blade stock. You can usually pick up a broken blade section from a local machine shop. Shape the blade first by grinding a tang on one end like a file tang. Then make the handle to suit your hand. If you have never used a long-handle knife you should give it a try. Make the handle 6½ to 7-in. long to start with. Later, if you don't like it simply cut it off. Glue the tang end of the blade blank into the handle using epoxy glue. Finish grinding, shaping and sharpening the blade after the handle is attached. Two of the most useful blade shapes are shown.

Frank Pittman

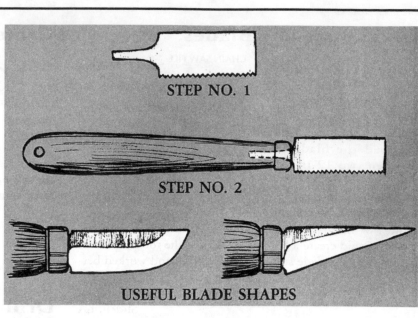

STEP NO. 1

STEP NO. 2

USEFUL BLADE SHAPES

An Oil Stone Retainer

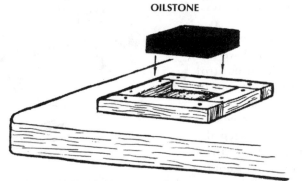

OILSTONE

An old technique used to prevent oil stones from being knocked off the bench is to simply attach four wooden strips to the bench top, forming a loose-fitting frame for the stone. This will not only retain the stone but it will allow you to easily turn the stone for use on edge or on the reverse side.

Frank Pittman

New Life for Tired Abrasives

When my abrasive belts and discs are not getting the job done, I no longer throw them out. Instead, I keep them right on the machine—belt or disc sander—and use them to shape scrapers and grind hatchets and heavy chisels. Aluminum oxide belts remove metal fast but don't overheat the steel. Try it and watch the sparks fly!

Ronald Hughes
Milford, OH

Sharpening on the Run

If you don't feel like lugging your sharpening stones around from job to job, carry a few sheets of 360 and 600-grit wet/dry silicon-carbide paper with you instead. Lay them on a piece of plate glass or other flat surface and wet them down with a lubricant such as oil, water or kerosene. Then hone our tools just as you would on an oil or water stone. By wrapping a strip of sandpaper around a dowel, you've got an instant slip stone for sharpening gouges.

Howard Ires
Danbury, CT

A Sharpening Aid

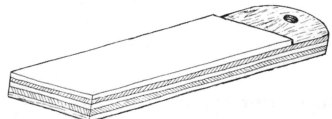

The strop that I use most often for the final stage in sharpening is one made from a piece of abrasive-coated leather glued to a ¾-in. plywood backing. Titebond glue can be used to laminate the leather to the plywood and the assembly can be clamped together in a woodworker's vise to dry. The size of the strop is up to you. Mine is approximately 2-in. wide and 8-in. long. Rub the surface of the leather with some fine abrasive powder. I use 600-grit silicon-carbide powder. This abrasive coating will actually cause the cutting edge to be polished.

Frank Pittman

Jack of Shims

We make a lot of jigs here and are constantly in need of shim stock. However, anything less than $1/8$-in. thick is hard to come by around a shop, so I've turned to old playing cards, which I find invaluable for this purpose. The cards are solid (compared to cardboard) and each one is a consistent thickness—about 10 thousandths (0.01 in.)

Howard Gaston
Naples, FL

Save the Band-Aids

When wood carving, I protect my thumb from my razor-sharp knives with a finger cut from a glove. A $2 pair of canvas and leather work gloves gives me 10 thumb protectors. I also find these protectors help me better grip the work.

Stan Borup
Covinga, CA

New Life for Broken Stones

Before discarding a broken sharpening stone, try gluing the pieces back together with epoxy. I've done this to several different stones in the past six years and, to date, none of the joints has failed.

Robert M. Vaughan
Roanoke, VA

Home-made Honing Guide

Holding a plane iron at a constant angle while honing can make all the difference in obtaining a keen edge. Here's a quick and inexpensive jig, made from a 6-in. stove bolt, two washers and two nuts. It will hold a plane iron at a steady angle without rocking. Pass the bolt through the hole in the plane iron with a nut and washer on each side of the blade. When adjusted to the proper angle, tighten the nuts to hold the setting.

James R. Krause
Skaneateles, NY

Alcohol in the Shop?

No, not that kind, but alcohol swabs are one of the handiest items in my shop. I use them for removing pencil lines; wiping graphite off drafting tools; cleaning adhesive off sanding pads and removing residues from tools. They will not raise the grain as water does, and they're ideal for cleaning smudges off a wood surface prior to finishing. I even use them as an antiseptic for the inevitable nicks and scratches. $1.39 for a box of 100 at my local drug store is a bargain.

Richard Reimers
West Seneca, NY

Checkmating the Checks

Anyone who works with green wood knows how rapidly it can dry out—checking along the way. My solution is to put the freshly cut chunks in plastic garbage bags, and then add wet saw dust. I seal the bag with the ties provided and set it in a cool place. In hot weather, you might add a couple of handfuls of salt to discourage mold.

Boles Derenda
West Seneca, NY

Layout and Gauges

Finding Center Fast

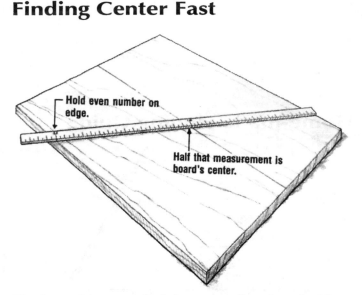

Hold even number on edge.

Half that measurement is board's center.

Here's a quick way to find the center of any board without having to divide fractions. Lay your rule or tape across the board on an angle and line up any even number on the board's edge. The center of the board will automatically be half that distance. For example, if you hold 20 in. on the edge, the center will be at 10 in. If you hold 26 in. on the edge, the center will be at 13 in. The only thing to watch: Always work from the same side of the rule or tape or it will throw your measurement off.

Eli Wengerd
Wilmot, OH

See-Through Patterns

To prolong the life of my paper patterns I trace them onto clear plastic with a black marking pen. I've found that 8-mil all-purpose vinyl covering works best. It's inexpensive and widely available in drug stores. An advantage of see-through patterns is that you can arrange the grain direction to match the project.

Jerry Cozzen
Anchorage, AK

Improvised Protractor

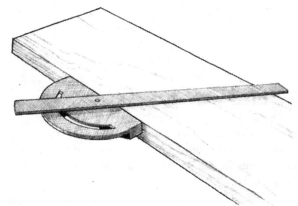

When you don't have a sliding I bevel or protractor handy, flip over the tablesaw's miter gauge and use it instead. You can set and lock any angle you want.

Bill Bigelow
Surry, NH

Quick Division

To quickly mark off equal divisions on a board for dovetails or other joints, place a rule diagonally across the surface so you can mark off the number of divisions in whole numbers. For example, to divide a board into 7 equal parts, place the zero mark on one edge 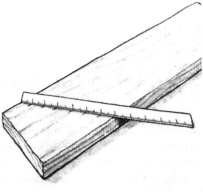 of the board and place the 7-in. mark on the other edge. Make a pencil mark at each inch mark—1 through 6—to divide the board.

Bill Bigelow
Surry, NH

Handy Marking Gauge

A 4-in. machinist's square is easily adapted to double as a marking gauge. Use a fine, triangular file to cut a small V-groove in the center of one end of the sliding rule. Put a pencil or steel scribe in this notch and, using the square's head as a guide, draw your layout lines.

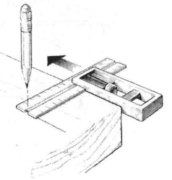

Donald Kinnaman
Phoenix, AZ

The Simplest Compass

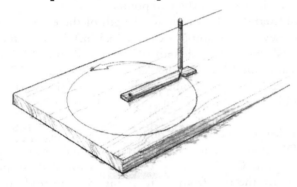

You can make a compass in a hurry by cutting a notch in one end of a stick of any length and driving a tack or small nail in the other end. Hold down the tack with one hand, and hold a pencil in the notch with the other hand, as you draw the circle. It works a lot better than a piece of string.

Mike Engstrom
Grand Forks, ND

Eternal Scribe

Years ago I worked with an old pattern maker who was never without his "scribe." This was just a draftsman's mechanical pencil with the lead replaced by a 3/32-in. drill bit. He had ground a sharp point on the chuck end of the bit for scribing lines. I liked his idea so much that I always have a similar scribe in my apron pocket. When not in use I retract the point for safekeeping.

Craig Bentzley
Chalfont, PA

Versatile Marking Gauge

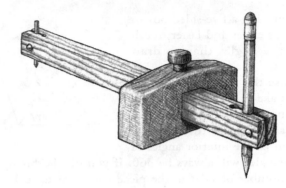

You can make your marking gauge more versatile by drilling a hole in it to hold a pencil. Drill the end opposite the scribing point and saw a kerf as shown. Drive in a screw so you can tighten the grip on the pencil. When a scribe mark won't do, you can stick in your pencil and use the pencil end of the gauge.

Simon Watts
San Francisco, CA

Handy Layout Fluid

A felt-tip permanent marker works as well as machinist's layout fluid for laying out marks on machines or tools. Rub the felt-tip marker over the whole area where you need to scribe a mark, let dry for about 30 seconds, and scribe into the ink from the marker. The ink can be removed with steel wool or alcohol when you're finished.

Robert Pauley
Decatur, GA

Hand-cut Dovetail Gauge

If you cut a lot of dovetails by hand, make your own layout gauge. Use hardwood for the fence and Plexiglas, phenolic, aluminum, brass or even thin hardwood or hardwood plywood for the blade. Cut both sides of one end of the blade to the angle you prefer for your dovetails. Leave the other end straight for use as a square. Glue and/or screw the fence to the blade, and make it all as precise and square as you can.

Frank Wright
Holland, MI

Calculating Perfect Pentagons

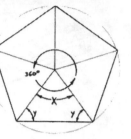

When making a five-sided box or frame, it's easier and faster to calculate the angles than to draw them out.

Picture the figure you are trying to make as a series of triangles that come together at a common point, as shown in the drawing. The sum of the interior angles of these triangles will always be 360. If you divide this figure by the number of sides in the piece you want to make (in this case five), you will get the number of degrees in the interior angle of one of the triangles (X). In the example in the drawing, the figure would be 72. The three interior angles of a triangle must always add up to 180, so the two outside angles CY) must be 180-72=108deg. Since these two angles are equal, each one must be 108deg. divided by 2, or 54deg. You can use the same calculation for a figure with any number of sides provided they are equal in length.

David Firth
Amherst, Nova Scotia, Canada

Seeking Circle Centers

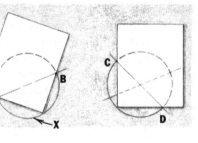

To find the center of a circle, position a postcard or sheet of paper so one corner touches the circumference (X in the drawing). Mark the points where the circle crosses the edges of the sheet (A and B in the drawing) and join the points with a straight line. Pick another section of the circle and repeat the process (C and D in drawing). The intersection of the two lines always gives the exact center of the circle.

Wesley Leinbach
Myerstown, PA

Drawing Fair Curves

Ever tried drawing a fair curve with a sprung batten and ended up holding the pencil with your teeth? Next time, try compressing the batten with a pipe or bar clamp. Increase the pressure, and the curvature becomes sharper. When it has the right curve, lay the batten on the paper or project. Now you can draw the line with a hand to spare.

Alison Weatherly
Berkeley, CA

String-Loop Ellipse

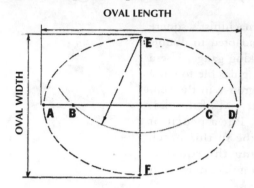

Most people know that ovals or ellipses can be drawn using a loop of string that revolves around two fixed points. However you may not know how to choose the fixed points to draw an oval the size you want.
Here's how to find the two points.
1. Determine the width and length of the ellipse you wish to draw. (For example we'll use 7x5 in.) 2. Draw the horizontal line AD the length of the oval (7 in.) 3. Draw the vertical line EF perpendicular to and through the center of line AD. Line EF should be the length of the desired oval's width (5 in.) divided equally on either side of line AD. 4. Set a divider to one half the length of AD ($3^1/2$ in.). Place one leg of the divider at point E or F and swing across line AD at points B and C. 5. Insert a small nail or pin at points B, E and C. Tie a loop of string around these points. Remove the nail from point E and you are ready to draw your oval.

James W. & Michael J. Bernthal
St. Louis, MO

Bisect an Angle
Without a Compass

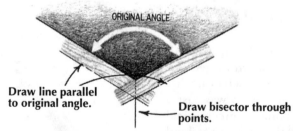

I have a very simple method for bisecting angles for mitering moldings. First I lay a parallel-sided board along one side of the angle and draw a line parallel to that side. Next, I lay the board along the other side of the angle and draw a similar line intersecting the first line. Finally, I connect the intersection of the two lines with the point of the original angle. The method is particularly useful for mitering baseboards in a room with odd angles.

J.A. Wilson
Lexington, MA

Equal Division Layout Device

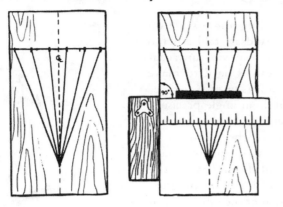

I learned this technique from a guitar maker and the concept has proven useful for a number of jobs. Guitar makers and repairmen need to be able to lay out six equal divisions for the guitar's nut. Nut lengths are not the same so a sliding scale like the one shown here works beautifully. To make this device, simply draw a line square with an edge across the blank. A small scrap of 1/4-in. birch plywood makes a good blank. Divide this line into the number of equal divisions needed by measuring with some convenient dimension, say 1/2 in. Locate the center of the divided line and drop a perpendicular line down to a point a convenient distance away. Draw lines from this point to each of the division marks on the first line. You can now lay a square on the edge of the jig and place the part to be divided on the blade of the square and slide it up or down to locate it's length. Equal divisions can now be marked on the part.

Frank Pittman

A Perfect Oval

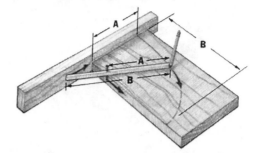

To draw a perfect oval (ellipse) of a given length and width, I make a template of one quarter of the ellipse, as shown in the drawing. Keep the near end of the stick in contact with the straightedge and the projecting nail in contact with the edge of the template stock while drawing the pencil-end of the stick through the elliptical arc.

John Wilson
Lexington, MA

Center Finder

To find the center of a circle, I sometimes use a framing square together with a combination square, as shown in the drawing. Make sure the combination square's ruler bisects the framing square's right angle; make two intersecting lines to locate the center of the circle.

John Roccanova
Ancramdale, NY

Laying Out Large Arcs

When an arc has a very gentle curve, it may be easier to lay it out from the span and rise instead of from the radius. You'll need two sticks and few nails. First lay out the span, AC, the midpoint, B, and the rise, E, directly above B. Next add D directly above A so that AD also equals the rise. Drive nails part way in at A, C, D and E. Take two sticks, each few inches longer than EC, and nail them to each other, one along DE and the other along EC as shown. Nail the sticks securely so the angle between them doesn't change. Put your pencil in the angle where the two sticks join and slide the sticks through one half of the arc and then the other half. Hold the sticks against the nails at A and E and then against the nails at E and C.

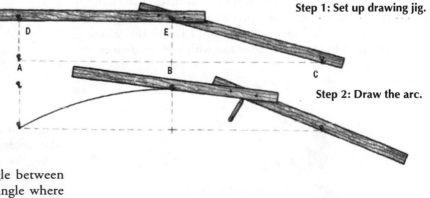

Step 1: Set up drawing jig.

Step 2: Draw the arc.

Angelo Rotundo
Pueblo, CO

Dowels Mark the Spot

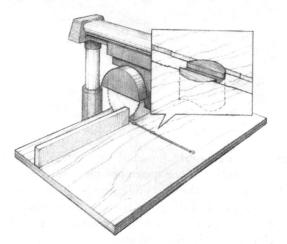

The table "rut" made by a radial arm saw blade is rarely an accurate indicator for precision trimming. It's also inadequate as a measuring point for cutoff setups.

About 3/4 in. from the fence, drill a 3/8-in. dia. hole clear through the table. Drill another hole about 1/3 the length of the "rut" and another hole at the end of the saw's travel. Drive in short dowels flush with the tabletop, and run the saw across the ends of the dowels. The kerf shows exactly where the blade is currently cutting. When the dowels get rough, drive new ones down on top of the old ones, and the old ones will fall out the bottom of the table.

With this setup, you don't have to pull out a still-coasting blade to measure where the blade is cutting. This saves measuring tapes, and probably, other things.

Bob Vaughan
Roanoke, VA

Circular Saw Gauge

I often use a straightedge combined with a circular saw to make accurate cuts. The set-up tool illustrated enables me to position the straightedge precisely before making the cut—whichever side I'm working from. I found this gauge so useful that I made another for use with various diameter router bits.

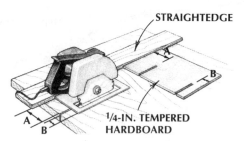

STRAIGHTEDGE

A
B

A
B
1/4-IN. TEMPERED
HARDBOARD

Edwin Perry
Albany, CA

Tilting the Bandsaw Table

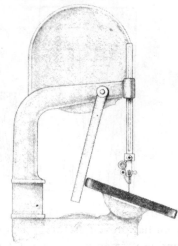

The tilting angle scale on most bandsaw tables is too small to read with any accuracy, so it's hard to make fine adjustments or re-establish an angle precisely. I attached a steel rule to the frame of the bandsaw as shown and can now make fine adjustments to the angle of tilt by reading the position of the table in relation to the rule. I can also re-establish any given angle by noting the distance on the scale or by attaching a piece of tape to its surface.

John Timby
Deming, NM

Masking-Tape Shims

When cutting tenons on the tablesaw, you often need to move the fence just a hair to adjust the thickness of the tenon. Instead of trying to adjust the fence in such tiny increments, I apply layers of tape to the side of my tenoning jig where it bears against the fence. Masking tape works well for a fairly thick shim, and mylar packing tape works as a very thin shim.

Ben Ericson
Eutaw, AL

Transferring Angles

I adjust my tablesaw bevel angle, miter-gauge angle and other angle adjustments on machines without actually measuring the angles. I set a draftsman's adjustable triangle to the angle as shown in the drawing. I then adjust the blade tilt or miter gauge to the adjustable triangle. If I'm working by hand, I transfer the angle directly to the stock.

Ric Hanisch
Quakertown, PA

Getting the Right Angle

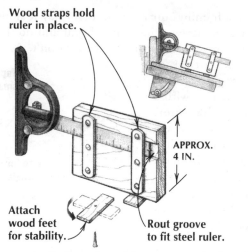

Wood straps hold ruler in place.

APPROX. 4 IN.

Attach wood feet for stability.

Rout groove to fit steel ruler.

The protractor built into the table support of a bandsaw or disc sander gives only an approximation of the angle of tilt. Needing greater precision, we adapted a machinist's protractor by adding a hardwood block as shown. This tool, called a "revolving turret protractor head," is made by Starrett. It's available through mail-order suppliers.

Edward Bartunek & Frank Bates
Hiram, OH

Make Your Own Grid

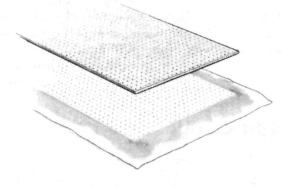

Scale plans are often drawn on a grid of square lines so you can readily enlarge the original drawing. But enlarging means redrawing the grid to a larger scale—a tedious and time-consuming job. I've found a quick way to do this with 1/8-in. Masonite Peg-Board. I place the Peg-Board over the paper I am using for the enlarged drawing, then I lightly spray the surface with paint. I end up with a pattern of dots that form the intersections of an exact, 1/2-in. grid.

I can reuse the Peg-Board several times, but switching colors helps me see if I've covered the board completely and not missed any of the dots. I make a supply of this "graph" paper for future use, as well as for the current project.

Dean St. Clair
Salesville, OH

Blade-Height Scale

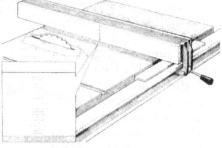

I had this idea for marking a scale on the side of a table-saw fence so I can set the saw blade at the exact height I want. So, I mark my fence with a knife in inches. I also marked the other side of the fence so I can set the height of my router bit when I mount my router on that side of the table.

Yeung Chan
Millbrae, CA

Tool Setting Scale

I use a see-through scale that I made from Lucite for setting the depth-of-cut for router bits, saw blades and similar tools. It's easy and accurate to use because the marks are on the side of the Lucite that is against the cutter. The Lucite is so clear that it's like having the marks suspended in midair. Make it any size you like, and use whatever pattern of marks you prefer. Scribe the marks in the Lucite, and then if you want them bolder, go over them with a felt-tip pen and rub off the excess ink. If you label the marks, be sure to put the labels on the side of the Lucite opposite to the marks so they don't appear backward when you use the scale.

Iron-On Patterns

Transfer patterns—such as carving or bandsaw patterns—onto the wood by copying the pattern on a photocopying machine, placing the copy face down on the wood, and ironing the back of the paper. This transfers the pattern to the wood. Of course, the pattern will be a mirror image of the pattern in the book. Patterns may be enlarged or reduced on the copying machine.

Bill Bigelow
Surry, NH

Hang That Square

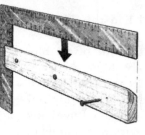

The accuracy of framing squares is not improved by dropping. To protect my squares and to store them conveniently, I devised a holder. I cut a piece of 1x3 the same length as the inside of the longer leg of the square and sawed a 45 degree bevel along one edge. I then nailed the strip to the wall within easy reach of my bench.

Jim Allder
Pearland, TX

Squaring a Square

To check a framing square for accuracy, lay it along the side of a board and draw a line. Then flip it and do the same. If the lines coincide, all's well. But if they don't...?

Lay the corner of the square on an anvil and tap the face with a ball-peen hammer. Hitting it close to the outside corner reduces the angle; tapping near the inside corner increases it.

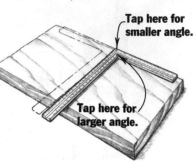

Tap here for smaller angle.

Tap here for larger angle.

Hugh Lineback
Siloam Springs, AR

Angles From Squares

You don't need to be a mathematician to lay out accurate angles in the shop. If you have a calculator with trig functions (sin, cos, tan, etc.), here's how to do it. Enter the angle that you want to lay out (say 37 degrees), hit the button labeled tan, read the value (in this case 0.75355) and move the decimal point over one place to the right (in this case to 7.5355). Now find 10 in. on one leg of your framing square and 7.5355 in. ($7^1/2$ in., or $7^{17}/32$ in. to be more precise) on the other leg of the square, and you have the angle as shown.

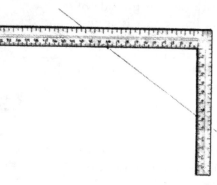

Trebor Narom
Onaled, NM

Shelf Support Holes

A fast, accurate method of drilling matching holes for adjustable shelves is to use a strip of Peg-Board. These holes are spaced on $1/2$-in. centers so you may have to skip one or more holes to get the spacing you want.

To avoid drilling in the wrong holes while thinking about tonight's dinner, run a strip of masking tape over the holes and circle the ones you plan to drill with a felt-tipped pen. When through with that set-up, pull off the tape.

Larry Humes
Bellingham, WA

No-Fault Hole Spacing

I recently made a kitchen cabinet with adjustable shelves. I had to space the shelf support pins exactly the same or the shelves would wobble. My solution was to buy a 4-ft.-long piano hinge which has holes on 2-in. centers. I opened the hinge flat, lined it up with the edge of the cabinet and clamped it. Then I marked the center of the holes with a spring-loaded drill guide called a Vix bit (available from Woodworker's Supply, 1108 N. Glenn Rd., Casper, WY 82601, 800-645-9292). Make sure you orient the hinge so that the same end is down each time—the spacing of the first hole may not be the same at both ends.

Howard Kovarsky
Spokane, WA

Height Gauge

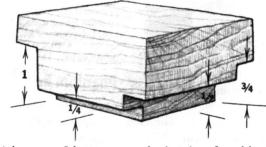

1

1/4

1/2

3/4

The quickest way I know to set the height of a tablesaw (or router) is with gauge blocks. I made this one from a 3-in. length of 2x4 cut to the settings I most frequently use. If you need more settings use another block. You can use this gauge block equally well for setting the distance of the fence to the saw blade.

L.T. Murphy
Oak Ridge, TN

Non-Slip Tools

Tools for striping, drawing, and measuring are often difficult to hold with one hand. To prevent slipping and increase ease of handling, take an old car innertube and make punchings with a paper punch. These punchings may be located to suit your needs. Secure to drafting instruments with a drop of super glue. Trim off the excess innertube from the tool at an angle. These tools can now be used for inking since they are now raised.

Jay Wallace
Ashland, OR

Power-Erase Layout Lines

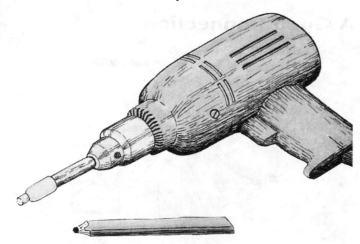

Most woodworking projects require layout lines for precision sawing, drilling, joining, and other operations. These lines should be removed before sanding and finishing. Cut this step to effortless seconds by using an eraser bit in your electric dill, which you can make from a plastic, tube-type eraser, available in any office-supply store. To add rigidity and eliminate wobble, cut the tube and eraser in half, and keep the extra half of the eraser as a refill.

Jerry Lyons

Centering Jig

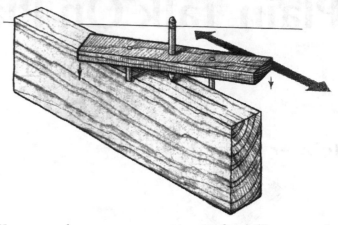

You can make your own centering jig for drilling or marking. Bore three evenly spaced holes through a piece of scrap wood in a straight line. The distance between the outer holes must be greater than the width of the stock you want to center on. Glue short dowels in the outer two holes (1/4-in. dia. is appropriate, but use whatever you have.) For marking, the center hole should be sized to hold your pencil snugly. For centering a drill bit, the center hole must be the same diameter as the drill bit. To use the jig, place it on the stock so the dowels are over the edges and twist it until the dowels touch the edges. You can slide it along to mark a centered line.

J.A. Wilson
Lexington, MA

Tape Measure Turned Note Pad

Have you ever noticed how easy it is to erase pencil marks from plastic laminate? A wet thumb will do it. I peeled off the label from my tape measure and glued a round scrap of plastic laminate in its place with contact cement. Now whenever I measure anything, I've got a handy spot to jot down the measurement.

Chris Carey
Houston, TX

Transferring Patterns

A quick way to transfer patterns from paper to wood is with a dressmaker's tracing wheel—available from fabric or sewing supply stores. Mounted on a handle, this miniature toothed wheel leaves small prick marks in the wood that are easily darkened with a pencil.

Jack Fleming
Poulsbo, WA

Plain Talk On Planing

Jointer Plane Jointer

Here's a way to joint pieces of wood that are too short to be run safely over the jointer. Flip your hand jointer plane upside down and clamp it in your bench vise. Now you can pass the wood over the plane to joint the edge. It's a good idea to use a push stick so that you don't nip your fingers on the blade.

Alan McMaster
Brighton, MI

Setting Knives by Magnet

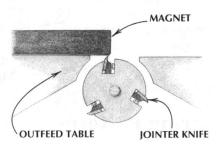

For years I've set the knives in my vintage jointer using a couple of magnets salvaged from two large stereo speakers. I set the magnets on the jointer's outfeed table, where it can hold each knife by its sharp edge. Run a strip of electrical tape across the contact area so you don't dull the knife.

Joseph Kosnosky
Friedens, PA

Roller Skate Rollers

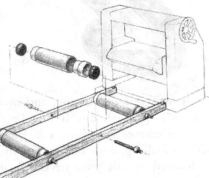

I made outfeed rollers for my planer from old-fashioned steel roller skate wheels, which have the same diameter as the outside of $1^{1}/_{2}$-in. plastic drain pipe. The drawing shows how I adapted the wheels to 2-in. plastic pipe. The ball-bearing roller skate wheels run very smoothly.

Robert Schroeder
Sheboygan Falls, WI

A Good Connection

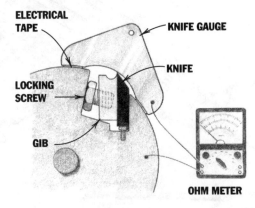

When setting a new knife in a planer or jointer, it's hard to determine the exact point at which the edge of the knife first touches the gauge. My solution is a simple one: Insulate the ends of the gauge with electrical tape and then hook an ohm meter to the gauge and planer as shown. Set the blade in place and slowly raise it until you make contact. If you don't have an ohm meter, a flashlight battery wired to a bulb is equally effective.

C.E. Rannefeld
Decatur, AL

Renewing Feed Rollers

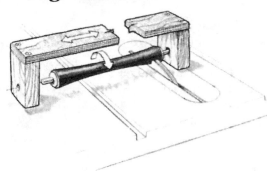

After 10 years of service the rubber feed rollers on my Makita planer were worn badly in the middle. This put uneven pressure on the stock causing it to slip. Replacement rollers cost around $300 so I decided to fix mine myself. I removed a roller and inserted the ends of the shaft in holes drilled in hardwood blocks. Then I put a 3/4-in. dado head in the tablesaw and gradually raised it until the teeth just grazed the surface at one end of the roller. After starting the saw I rotated the roller against the direction of cut, removing as little roller stock as possible, until I had a clean, uniform cylinder.

Ben Erickson
Eutaw, AL

End Grain Cutting Boards

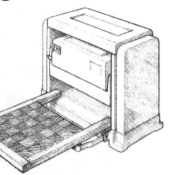

When making end grain cutting boards 10 in. or 12 in. square, I surface them in a thickness planer. However, this can be dangerous: If the surface of the cutting board is uneven (as it's likely to be), the infeed rollers may not adequately grab the wood before the planer knives strike it. If this happens, the board can come flying back at you. To prevent this, I glue wood strips to each side of the board. The strips extend about 1/8 in. above the surface of the cutting board and about 6 in. beyond the front edge of the board. This gives the rollers something solid to hold onto as the board feeds through the planer. I also glue a strip to the rear edge of the board so the knives don't tear out the grain at the rear edge of the cutting board. I leave the three strips on until I've finished sanding and then bandsaw them off.

Todd Bayer
Bethel, VT

Making the Most of Your Inca

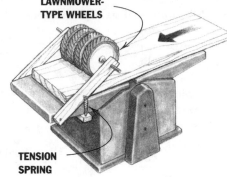

LAWNMOWER-TYPE WHEELS

TENSION SPRING

My Inca planer-jointer has such a short bed that I find it difficult to hold long boards flat. So I rigged a pivot and four rubber-tired wheels that ride on top of the board. Springs from an old army cot provide downward pressure. An added benefit of this rig is that you can keep your hands clear of the cutter knives.

James Watson
Atlanta, GA

Machine Jointing End Grain

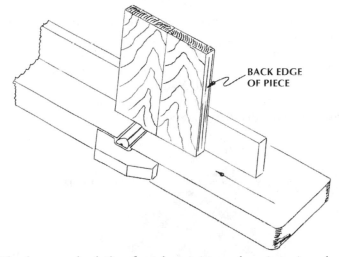

BACK EDGE OF PIECE

The best method I've found to joint end grain using the jointer is to size the given panel down to within 1/16 in. oversize at each end and allowing an 1/8 in. extra at the back edge. (Usually there is an edge that is not seen as much as the opposite edge or front edge.) After jointing each "end" at the allowed 1/16 in., you may then rip or joint the back edge to remove whatever chipout that occurred in the jointing process. As you're jointing, slow down the feed as you near the back edge and the chipouts will be minimal. Of course, the knife sharpness as well as how steady you handle the piece will affect the quality and accurateness of this operation. NOTE: caution should be exercised in the judgement of the smallest width pieces that should be safely jointed. Your actual width dimensions will depend on the size jointer you have available to use.

Jerry Lyons

4x4 Push Block

I use this 12-in.-long 4x4 as a push block when jointing small pieces. This not only gives me better control, but the weight helps prevent kickback. Also, the push block has a sacrificial wood catch on the end (see drawing) which is easy to replace should it get cut by the jointer knives.

A stud and wing nut hold this sacrificial catch to the end of the 4x4. And I cut the hole in the catch off center so that the catch has two positions—one for pushing thick stock, the other for thin stock.

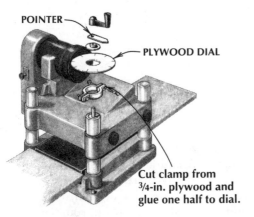

SACRIFICIAL END PIECE

Rout finger grips above fence.

Chip Coffin
Sunnyvale, CA

Turn-Around Planer

Wooden peg locks rotating planer table in place.

To make the best use of shop space, I mounted my portable planer under my bench and installed rollers at each end of the bench so I could plane long boards without moving the machine. This worked well, but it still meant I needed to carry all the stock from the outfeed side to the infeed when making several passes. One day I got smart and mounted the planer on a piece of plywood with a "lazy Susan" underneath. Wooden pegs keep it locked in position. Now all I have to do is pull the pins and rotate the planer 180 degrees for the second pass.

Chuck LeDoux
Heppner, OR

Planer Depth Gauge

Thickness gauges on planers are notoriously unreliable, so I made my own accurate to $1/64$-in. First I cutout a plywood dial, the same size as the inside diameter of the adjusting wheel. Then I made two clamp brackets and glued one to the underside of the dial. You could use the wheel handle itself as a pointer or install one under the wheel nut as I did. Paint the dial flat white for easy reading.

POINTER

PLYWOOD DIAL

Cut clamp from $3/4$-in. plywood and glue one half to dial.

To calibrate the dial, measure the distance between minimum and maximum depth of cut. (Suppose it comes to $5^1/4$-in.) Divide by the number of complete turns of the handle. (Let's say 35.) The answer ($5/32$ in.) tells you how far one complete turn of the handle raises or lowers the knives. Use a compass to divide the dial's perimeter into 10 equal segments. Each one will represent $5/32$ divided by 10, or $1/64$ in.

Ernest Barta
St. Petersburg, FL

Planing Thin Stock

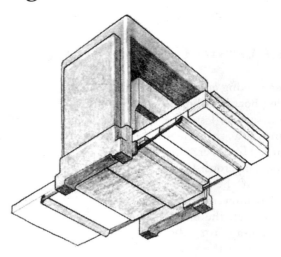

The instructions on my Ryobi/Sears 10-in. planer say that planing stock less than $1/2$-in. thick is not recommended. I need a lot of lumber that is thinner than $1/2$ in., so I made a jig that inserts in the planer and allows me to plane stock as thin as $1/8$ in.

The jig is 10 in. wide and 26 in. long. I made mine from $3/4$-in. medium density fiberboard (MDF), which I varnished to make a smooth surface. Hardwood plywood would work, too. I fastened two wooden cleats across one end of the jig to fit over the roller on the input side.

John Neumann
Sauk Centre, MN

Lazy (Susan) Planing

When planing a number of boards on my small thickness planer, I got tired of carrying the boards around from the outfeed end to the infeed end. Instead, I rotate the planer 180 degrees on a heavy-duty lazy-susan bearing and run the boards back through to where they started. I mounted the bearing between two squares of 3/4-in. plywood and installed a removable pin to lock the planer in position while in use.

Thomas Whalen
Cohoes, NY

Handy Source for Rollers

Before dishing out $15 or $20 for an outfeed roller, try the local print shop. Ask for "distributor," "ductor" or "rider" rollers. These usually have a built-in shaft, a soft rubber coating and a length of 10 in. or more. What you don't want are oscillating rollers or ones that need a shaft.

Tom White
Latham, NY

Quick-Adjust Bed-Roller Shims

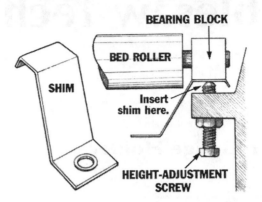

Setting planer bed rollers low (.002 to .006 in. above the bed) gives a super smooth surface for a final cut. But when surfacing rough lumber, you want the rollers higher so you don't have a tug of war trying to pull stock through the planer.

Make the bed rollers easy to adjust by making four shims from .015 in. steel shim stock (available from Small Parts, Inc., 6891 NE Third Ave., P.O. Box 381736, Miami, FL 33238). Alternatively, 26-, 27- or 28-gauge sheet metal will also work fine. The drawing shows the shims I made for my Powermatic 100 12-in. planer. The little turndown on the end keeps the shim from backing out and may or may not be necessary on your planer.

Reach under the bed, raise the bed roller bearing block and simply insert the four shims over the tops of the four height-adjustment screws. The shims allow you to set your bed rollers low for fine work and quickly jack them up .015 in. for rough work. Remove the shims for the last two passes and, like magic, you'll get a smooth cut.

Robert M. Vaughan
Roanoke, VA

Tablesaw Techniques

Miter-Gauge Holder

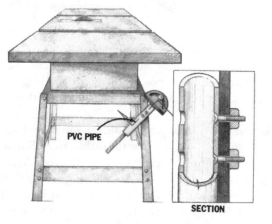

I needed a handy place to put my tablesaw miter gauge when it wasn't in use. I fastened a 12-in. length of PVC pipe to the side of my tablesaw with 1/4-in. flat-head stove bolts through the pipe and the saw base. I drilled 1/4-in. holes through both sides of the pipe, then enlarged the holes in one side of the pipe enough for the bolt head and screwdriver to fit through. I countersank the inside of the holes on the opposite side of the pipe, so the bolt heads would be flush with the inside surface.

Blair Hubbard
Knoxville, MD

Magnet Stop Block

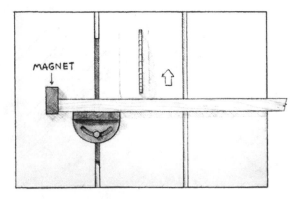

A strong magnet makes an excellent stop block for making multiple cross cuts if your tablesaw top is made of cast iron.

Bill Bigelow
Surry, NH

Miter-Gauge Fence and Stop

My miter-gauge auxiliary fence incorporates an adjustable stop that locks in place with wing nuts on 1/4 x 2-in. carriage bolts. I use a 3/4-in. plywood fence 3 in. wide by 40 in. long. The 1/4-in. wide slot for the carriage bolts ends 1 in. from the ends of the fence.

Bruce Levine
New York, NY

Crosscut Stop Block

When crosscutting on the tablesaw, it isn't safe to use the rip fence as a stop by butting the end of the workpiece against it. The cutoff can bind between the fence and the blade and kick back. But a stop is handy for crosscutting lots of same-length pieces.

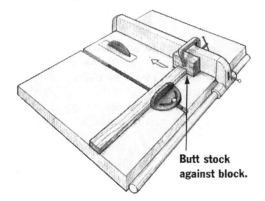

Butt stock against block.

I clamp a stop block to the fence well back from the blade. This leaves a safe gap between the end of the stock and the fence when I'm making the cut.

Alvin H. Sherwood
Round Lake, IL

Push-Stick/Hold-Down

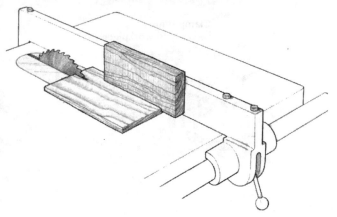

Keep narrow or thin pieces of wood under control and your fingers at a safe distance from the blade while ripping on the tablesaw with a combination push-stick/hold-down as shown in the drawing. The $^1/8$-in. to $^1/4$-in. heel catches the trailing end of the workpiece to push it through while the rest of the pusher holds the narrow piece of stock flat on the table.

Ric Hanisch
Quakertown, PA

Cleaning Gummy Blades

The tar and gum that build up on circular saw blades and router bits can increase friction, causing them to heat up and distort, and your wood to burn. The quickest and cheapest method I've found to remove these deposits is with Easy-Off oven cleaner. Just spray the blade or cutter, let it stand for a few minutes and then rinse it off with water. It works every time.

Cary Lowrance
Orland Hills, IL

Push-Stick Pointer

Cutting thin stock on the tablesaw can be hazardous. When ripping a number of thin strips, I use a special push stick with a needle-sharp finishing nail inserted in the end. The nail lets me apply pressure anywhere on the stock (not just at the end), so I can hold the stock firmly to the table while pushing it past

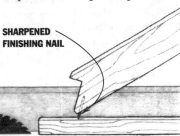

SHARPENED
FINISHING NAIL

the blade. The "pin prick" caused by the nail is so tiny that it disappears in the sanding and finishing process.

Tim Hanson
Indianapolis, IN

Anti-Kickback Hold-Down

I made a combination hold-down and anti-kickback device from a $^3/4$-in. thick piece of 4 by 4-in. hardwood. On one end, I made a 2-in. long slot cut at 45 degrees. It holds a piece of Lucite, phenolic or similar flexible material as shown in the drawing. You can shim it with layers of tape to get the fit that you want. I install it as needed on the top edge of my auxiliary fence with hanger bolts and wing nuts.

Paul Fertell
Chester Springs, PA

Low-Tech Blade Cleaner

The quickest and most effective way to clean blades that I know is to use a solution of household ammonia and cider vinegar (1 cup of cider vinegar to 1 quart of ammonia). First, I soak a blade in the solution for an hour or two then I lay it on a wad of newspaper and pour on a little of the mixture. Finally, spread the mixture with 000 steel wool and watch the tar and pitch melt away. After cleaning, dry the blade and wipe on a dry lubricant such as Dri-Cote.

Bob Colpetzer
Clinton, TN

Push-Stick Holder

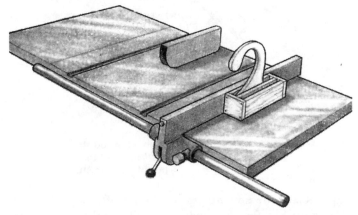

Make a push-stick holder from $^1/2$-in. plywood, and mount it to your rip fence with contact cement. The push stick is always where you need it.

Michael Carey
Houston, TX

Trimming Edge Banding

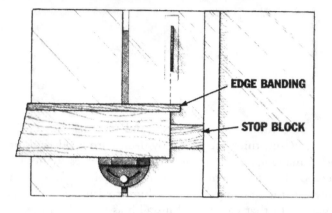

The drawing shows a setup I use to trim off the overhanging end of edge banding on plywood shelves and cabinet parts. Clamp a stop block against the fence so that the left-hand edge of the block lines up with the left-hand edge of the blade. Position the shelf against the stop block as shown, and use the miter gauge to guide the shelf through the cut. If you've set it up carefully, and your miter gauge is accurate, the saw will cut off the edge banding flush with the edge of the plywood.

Mark Sfirri
New Hope, PA

More on Push Sticks

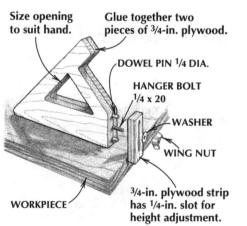

I appreciate the advantages of Chip Coffin's push stick (AW #39) but find my style of handle works better. Not only can I push the stock over the jointer (or past the saw blade); I can also bear down on the stock when necessary. At no time are my fingers anywhere near a cutting edge.

Charles Cox
Yukon, OK

Knife Edges on the Tablesaw

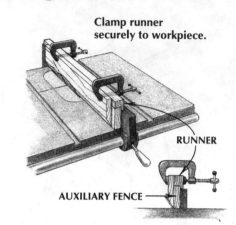

Cutting knife edges on the tablesaw is awkward because the edge tends to collapse or slip down into the table insert. My method works equally well whether the angle is only a few degrees or 45.

Yeung Chan
Millbrae, CA

Soaking Saw Blades

I tried Bob Colpetzer's low-tech blade cleaner with excellent results. The only problem was finding the right size and shape of container for the 10-in. circular saw blades. Rubbermaid to the rescue! Their 22-cup, No. 5 Servin' Saver comes in clear plastic, 11-in. dia., 4-in. high. The airtight cover seals in smells, so the ammonia can do its job without leaving an aroma in the shop.

Dick Applebaum
Tucson, AZ

Centering the Dado

When using an adjustable dado head I've had difficulty predicting the exact center of the cut. So I set the fence, started the saw and ran a piece of scrap over the blade. Then I marked the exact center of the cut and transferred the line to an adhesive label on the saw table. Whatever the width of the slot, the center will always be the same. This won't work with stacking dadoes because adding chippers or filler blades moves the center of cut to the left.

Oscar Williams
Lincoln, NE

Angled Cuts on Plywood

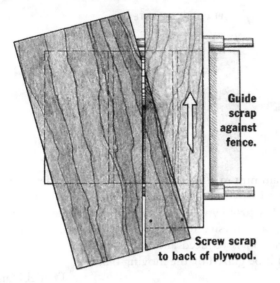

Guide scrap against fence.

Screw scrap to back of plywood.

To make angled cuts on large pieces of plywood, screw a scrap piece of ply to the back of the piece you want to cut. Guide the scrap along the tablesaw fence to make the cut.

Jeff Day
Perkasie, PA

Getting the First Edge Straight

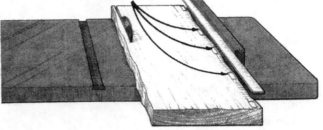

DOUBLE-SIDED TAPE

To get a straight edge on one side of a board that has two irregular edges, attach a straightedge to one side with double-sided tape. Then run it through the tablesaw with the straightedge against the fence. The tape won't damage the wood the way nails will.

Stan Watson
Palm Springs, CA

Leg-Tapering Jig

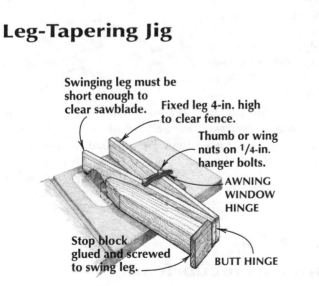

Swinging leg must be short enough to clear sawblade.

Fixed leg 4-in. high to clear fence.

Thumb or wing nuts on 1/4-in. hanger bolts.

AWNING WINDOW HINGE

Stop block glued and screwed to swing leg.

BUTT HINGE

This simple jig makes cutting consistent tapers on table legs easy and safe. If the leg is tapered for one-third of its length (or less), you can cut all four faces with one setting of the jig. For longer tapers, cut two adjacent tapers on each leg and then reset the angle to cut the remaining two.

Anthony Yackimowicz
Hazleton, PA

Tapering Jig

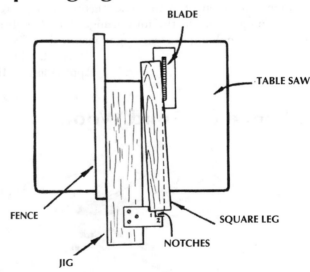

BLADE

TABLE SAW

FENCE

JIG

NOTCHES

SQUARE LEG

This jig is used for tapering a square leg. Place any side of the square stock in notch (1) of the jig. Push both the jig and the stock through the blade. Place an adjacent side of stock in the jig in notch (1) and repeat the operation. The two remaining sides should be cut in notch (2) in the same manner. It is important that the notches be exactly the same size.

Jay Wallace
Ashland, OR

Setting the Fence

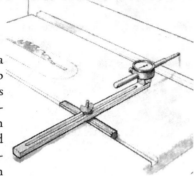

Long ago I bought a tablesaw that was so cheap that setting the fence was a hit or miss affair. I finally built the gauge shown here using scrap wood and a machinist's dial indicator. With this jig I can quickly position the fence so it's exactly parallel to the slots in the table.

Gordon Davis
Houston, TX

Aligning a Saw Fence

Here's a quick and easy way to align your tablesaw rip fence with a miter-gauge slot. Loosen the screws that lock the fence alignment, then press the fence against a long, steel rule or framing square in the miter-gauge slot. Re-tighten the screws while holding the fence tight against the rule.

David R. Johnson
Apple Valley, MN

Rip Fence for Solid Wood

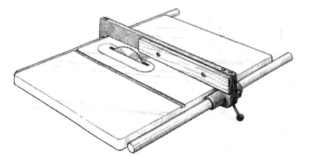

Wood often twists and bends when internal stresses are released during ripping. A rip fence that ends at the mid-point of the blade gives the wood room to do its own thing without binding between the fence and blade. I get the effect of a half-length fence by bolting a half-length board to the side of my full-length fence.

Jim Turbyville
Westland, MI

Facing the Fence

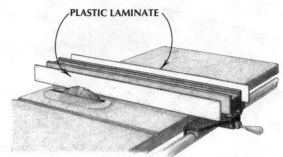

PLASTIC LAMINATE

Some aluminum fences have a nasty habit of leaving black smears when you run a piece of wood through the saw. To solve this problem, I attached pieces of plastic laminate with spray adhesive to both sides of the fence. A bonus is that friction is reduced and the laminate is easily replaced should it be grazed by the moving blade.

Daniel Haubert
Framington Hills, MI

Refacing Your Fence

If you've accidentally scarred your Biesemeyer fence with a moving saw blade, here's how to repair it: Remove the laminate from both sides of the fence and replace it with two pieces of 3/4-in. plywood, faced with white plastic laminate on both sides. Attach the plywood by driving 3 1/2-in. drywall screws through from the right side of the fence, so the

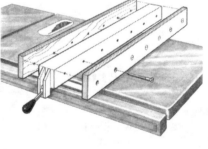

screws penetrate but don't protrude from the plywood on the left side. Countersink the heads flush. I made the new facings for my saw higher than the standard ones supplied by Biesemeyer. I find higher facings to be an advantage.

John Grew-Sheridan
San Francisco, CA

Cornstarch Lubricant

I recently learned that cornstarch makes an excellent lubricant. I keep some near the tablesaw in a shaker with a perforated lid. Now and then, I shake it over the table and fence, and voila!—the heaviest, roughest boards glide smoothly across the surface.

Margaret Scally
Albuquerque, NM

Sawing Thin Stock Safely

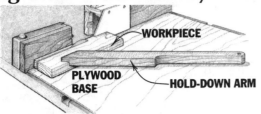

WORKPIECE

PLYWOOD BASE

HOLD-DOWN ARM

This simple jig replaces a push stick and takes the risk out of sawing slats or other thin stock. The base is made from 1/8-in. plywood and has a thin slot cut in it for the blade, to prevent off-cuts from falling into the blade slot. A U-shaped push stick fits over both the metal fence and an auxiliary wooden fence and has a thin, 1/16-in. laminated plastic face to push the stock past the blade. Finally, there's a long hold-down/anti-kickback arm that is notched as shown to keep the stock pressed firmly against the fence and table. I find I get the cleanest cuts by jointing the surface of the stock before cutting each slat.

Bob Barnes
Joplin, MO

Tablesaw as Jointer

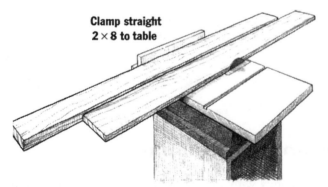

Clamp straight
2 × 8 to table

Here is a method I use to convert my tablesaw to a jointer with an effective bed length of 8 ft., I clamp a very straight and true 8 ft. 2x8 to the regular rip fence. With a triple-chip grind, 48-tooth carbide saw blade, I take shallow cuts about 1/16 in. or less. Bowed stock up to 10 ft. long can be easily straightened with several passes. Another advantage is that you don't have to worry about the direction of the grain as you would on a regular jointer. The 48-tooth blade produces a surface that is ready to glue without any planing. It's important to have a good extension table on the outfeed side of the table because it is essential that the stock pass through the saw blade without the slightest wobble— especially at the end of the cut. If I'm jointing boards for edge gluing, I've discovered that I get a better and flatter panel if I run every other board through the tablesaw/jointer face down.

Lyle E. Bohrer
Beaumont, TX

Stop the Rattle

To keep my tablesaw insert from vibrating and rattling, I put little dabs of Shoe Goo on the sides near the corners. Next I trimmed it to fit with a sharp knife after it has hardened. Shoe Goo is a soft plastic that comes in a tube.

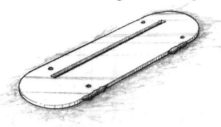

Runners use it to patch worn areas on the soles of running shoes. Athletic-wear stores carry it.

Brian Honey
Barrie, Ontario

No-Chip Crosscut Tip

If you've ever crosscut plywood on the tablesaw, you know that it usually splinters and leaves a bad edge on the bottom of the cut.

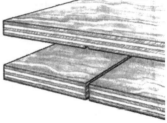

A good way to prevent this is to first make a shallow cut about 1/8-in. deep. Then raise the blade up enough to cut through the plywood, and make a second cut. You'll get a substantially cleaner cut, but you still should always keep the best side of the sheet facing up.

Patrick Russo
Pattersonville, NY

Cutting Plywood

Cutting a full 4x8 sheet of plywood on the tablesaw is an awkward job, even with two people. The miter gauge comes out of its slot, and the fence may not have enough travel. My solution is to clamp a 2x4 to the underside of the plywood and let it bear against the left-hand edge of the table. It should project beyond the plywood a couple feet on each side. The edge of the table on my Delta Unisaw is 18 in. from the blade, so I place the 2x4 exactly 18 in. from where I wish to cut. I find I can safely get a clean, accurate cut each time.

Paul Mueller
San Francisco, CA

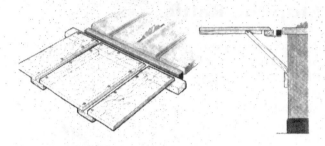

Drop-Down Feed Table

When ripping long planks I often found if I used a roller support it ended up in the wrong place—or I managed to tip it over. So I decided to make a hinged outfeed table that drops down out of the way when not in use. I first ripped a 20 by 24-in. piece of 1/2-in. plywood into three sections. Then I glued and screwed these to two 1x4 pieces of hardwood creating slots that matched the miter gauge slots on my tablesaw. I then hinged the whole assembly and attached it to the back edge of the saw table as shown. The final step was to bevel the front edge of the new outfeed table so a workpiece wouldn't hang up when I push it across. Two legs support the extension table when it's in use, then fold up and out of the way when it's down.

Derek Roff
Albuquerque, NM

Improved Feather Board

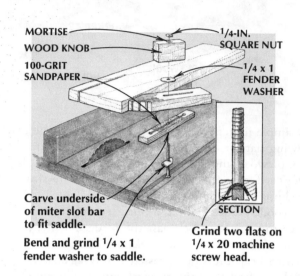

MORTISE

WOOD KNOB

100-GRIT SANDPAPER

1/4-IN. SQUARE NUT

1/4 x 1 FENDER WASHER

SECTION

Carve underside of miter slot bar to fit saddle.

Bend and grind 1/4 x 1 fender washer to saddle.

Grind two flats on 1/4 x 20 machine screw head.

The miter-slot feather board is a good idea but has some drawbacks: It's awkward to tighten and sometimes the screw turns with the wing nut. I settled this by grinding flats on the head of the screw, adding a saddle-shaped washer as shown and replacing the wing nut with a wood knob.

Frank Gregg
Dallas, TX

Using Cast-off Casters

Taking up space in my "junk drawer" were a quantity of heavy swivel casters with bolt ends. Since I needed a roller stand I drilled holes on 3-in. centers in a piece of angle iron and mounted the casters so they were all the same height. I then attached the back of the angle iron to a 2x6 and screwed the whole assembly to a sawhorse. I adjusted the height so the rollers were level with the tablesaw or a fraction below it. I use the stand not only when ripping, but when crosscutting long boards as well. The long row of casters gives just the added support needed.

Frank Mikus
Wecosville, PA

Lexan Feather Boards

I wasn't happy with any of my feather boards until I made one out of 1/4-in.-thick Lexan. This stuff is both flexible and virtually unbreakable. I started with a 3 by 8-in. piece, sawed one end at 45 degrees, and then kerfed the angled end on the tablesaw with a fine-tooth ATB blade. I extended the Lexan by adding a length of 3/4-in. plywood as shown in the drawing. I liked my feather board so well that I made another one, which mounts vertically on the fence to serve as a hold-down.

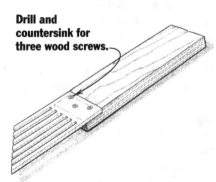

Drill and countersink for three wood screws.

Merle Hyldahl
Rochester, NY

No-Grope Switches

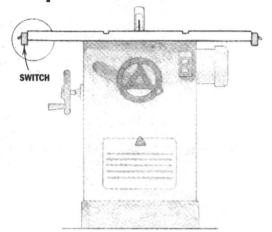

Because my 10-in. carpenters saw had the on/off switch mounted on the front of the base, I couldn't see the switch when cutting large stock and I had to blindly feel around for it. Exasperated, I mounted two, two-way switches, either side of the table, just below the surface. Now I can shut the saw off, with either hand, without having to grope around for a switch.

Lowell Reistad
Vashon, WA

No-Hands Stop Switch

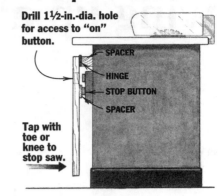

"No-Grope Switches" ("Tech Tips," AW #33) was useful but required additional switches and wiring, and you also have to take one hand off the work to trip the switch—a potential safety hazard. A better solution is to modify the existing switch so it can be operated by foot. Hinge a piece of 1x4, position a block to connect with the off switch and you're in business.

George Weber
Magalia, CA

Red Is for Danger

Saws don't care what they cut. As a reminder, I've highlighted the danger zones near my saw blades with bright red warning strips. I painted a band 6-in. long on each side of the blade of my radial arm saw. I then made a new insert for my table saw and painted that red, too. Finally, I masked off the rip fence and spray painted it 3 in. in front and 4 in. behind the blade as a reminder to use a push stick when I get that close.

Charles Hirsch
Brookville, OH

Warning! Blade Coming!

Cutoff boxes, tenoning jigs and similar fixtures can be dangerous if you forget that the blade is going to exit from the rear of the fixture. Glue a block with angled edges over the slot where the blade comes through. It will alert 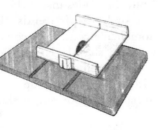 you to danger if your fingers stray too close while your attention is on the cut.

John Kriegshauser
Kansas City, MO

Scrap-Metal Splitter

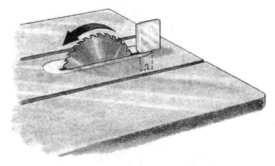

If you're like me, you run your tablesaw without a guard. When you remove the guard, you're also removing the splitter, which prevents kickback by keeping the saw kerf from closing. Rather than run the risk of kickback, I made my own splitter from a discarded 3/32-in. aluminum sign.

I cut the new splitter to the shape shown in the drawing, filed the leading edge to a slight taper, and cleaned up the burrs. When fastened to the splitter brackets, the splitter should exactly bisect the blade. If necessary, move it sideways by shimming it with thin metal washers. Before starting the saw, turn the blade around by hand, raising and lowering it to make sure it clears the splitter.

Dana Batory
Crestline, OH

Sawing up a Storm

Skilsaw Cut-Off

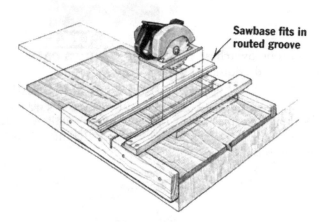

Sawbase fits in routed groove

This is a useful jig for anyone who does a lot of crosscutting of rough stock but doesn't own a radial arm or cut-off saw. I find it especially handy not to have to mount the skilsaw-it just drops into the wood guides—so it is always free for other uses. For my purposes a 24-in. by 48-in. base was convenient, but the dimensions can vary to suit individual needs.

Bruce Levine
New York, NY

More on Skilsaw Cut-Off Jig

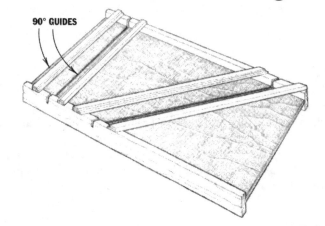

90° GUIDES

I made Bruce Levine's dandy jig (left) with the same size base, 24-in. by 48-in. Then I realized that if I moved the 90 degree guides down to the end of the base there was room enough for 45 degree guides as well. Left-handers can make 45 degree cuts from the near side of the jig, as it appears in the drawing. Right-handers work from the far side.

C.J. Ledoux
Heppner, OK

Sawing Stands

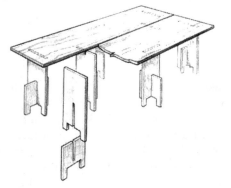

I use several easily made and easily disassembled particle-board stands to support plywood when sawing it with a portable saw. I get by with a minimum number by positioning them directly on the cut line. I saw right through the stands, which continue to support both sides of the cut.

Ron Pavelka
Orange, CA

Storing Small Blades

I keep all of my small blades (coping saw, scroll-saw, saber-saw, hack saw) organized and stored in short lengths of plastic pipe. I put the blades inside the pipes and cork one or both pipe ends. To keep these homemade containers convenient, I store them in slightly larger pieces of plastic pipe. I fasten the pipe sections to the wall with a screw at the top and a long screw or nail at the bottom, as shown.

Bill Houghton
Sebastopol, CA

Splinter-Free Plywood Cuts

The tendency of portable circular saws to splinter the top side of plywood can be minimized with the saw guide shown in the drawing. Make it out of two pieces of wood. The edge of the upper narrow piece must be dead straight. Fasten it to the lower piece, revealing a bit more than the width of the shoe of the portable saw so that the saw can be used to trim the piece to the right width. The lower piece holds down the wood fibers, preventing splintering.

Roland Filion
Manville, RI

Last Word on Stop Blocks

Everyone has their favorite style stop block. Here's mine.

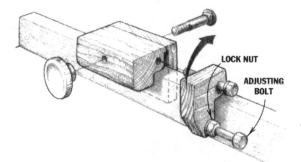

LOCK NUT

ADJUSTING BOLT

Slacking the large knob lets you move the block along your fence, while turning the machine bolt on the bottom of the stop fine-tunes adjustments. To give me greater control over adjustments, I drilled a $5/16$-in. hole for the adjusting bolt and then cut threads directly in the wood with a $3/8$-in. by 16 tap. That way, one full turn of the stop bolt equals $1/16$ in. and a quarter turn $1/64$ in. Using a hard, dense wood such as maple or walnut you'll never have a problem with stripped threads. You may wish to make a left-handed version or add a second flip up block to the one illustrated. You could then use it either side of the saw.

Eugene Paules
Shelton, CT

More on Stop Blocks

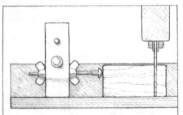
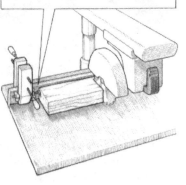

Instead of clamping a stop block to the fence on my radial arm saw, I use a modified 6-in. wooden hand screw. I roughly set the hand screw then fine-tune the position by moving the head of a $1/4$-in. round head machine screw that fits in a hole drilled in one arm of the clamp. Wing nuts on either side of the screw hold it in place once I've adjusted it.

I.R. Kevbane
Amarillo, TX

Micro-Adjustable Stop Block

A bolt screwed into a snug (but not tight) hole in a block of wood becomes a finely adjustable stop block with the added advantage that debris doesn't accumulate in front of the block.

Trebor Narom
Onajed, NM

Flip-Up Stop Block

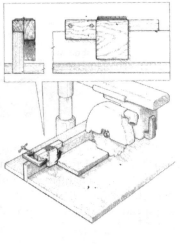

I always use this adjustable stop, made with a simple cabinet hinge, when cutting a number of pieces the same length on a radial arm or chop saw. I flip the stop up, square one end of the stock, then turn the workpiece around and trim it to length with the stop down. All I need to do to reposition the stop block is slack the clamp and slide it along the fence.

Richard Hooton
East Gadsen, AL

Damping Scroll-Saw Vibrations

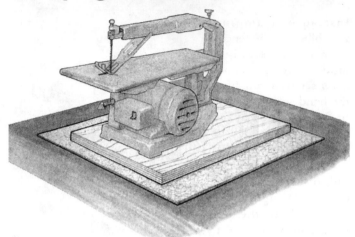

I didn't have room for a separate stand for my scroll saw, so I bolted it to a 3/4-in. plywood base. But when I used it on top of my workbench, it vibrated so much I had to clamp it to the benchtop. I solved the vibration problem by putting the saw on a routing/sanding pad—a foam pad (sold by woodworking-supply companies) for holding small items stationary. The pad keeps the scroll saw from "walking around" and dampens the vibrations. Now it's much easier to get accurate cuts.

Wayne Dragish
Linwood, PA

Reciprocating File

In these days of the scroll saw revolution, flea markets are chock full of old-style cast-iron jigsaws. I bought one recently and converted it to a reciprocating filing machine.

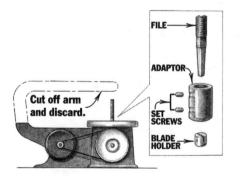

I first cut off the upper arm, and then I made an adaptor which held the file in place and fit over the jigsaw blade holder. I also changed the pulleys and found that a 1-in.-dia. pulley driving a 6-in.-dia. pulley will give the right filing speed, when driven by a 1,725-rpm motor.

Ron Pavelka
Orange, CA

Clamp Tether

When a blade snaps on my scroll saw, the blade clamps often go flying. When I got tired of chasing them all over the shop floor, I tethered them to the upper and lower saw arms with short pieces of mono-filament fishline.
George Weber
Brooklyn, NY

Miter Saw Table Extension

I like the portability of compound miter saws but find the base too small to conveniently crosscut long stock.

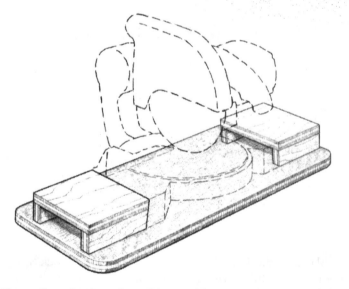

Extending the base by adding tables on either side of the saw blade greatly improves its usefulness. I made my extension table base out of 3/4-in. plywood, bolted the saw in place, then fitted the two side tables. The illustration is for an 8-in. Delta saw but the same idea would work for other brands. Incidentally, the saw doesn't have to be centered: you may want to make the left side table longer (or shorter) than the right. If you keep the overall length to 28 in. you can still carry the assembly sideways through doorways.

CharIes L. Alden
Burlington, NC

Squaring a Radial Arm Saw

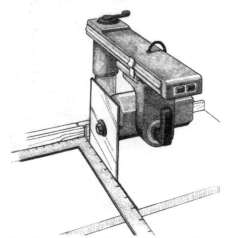

This jig takes the guesswork out of squaring a radial arm saw. Drill an arbor-size hole in the center of a piece of flat aluminum sheet stock that's about 8-in. square and at least 3/16-in. thick. Remove the blade and replace it with the aluminum square. You now have 8 in. to lay a framing square against—not just a couple of teeth.

Ron Tye
Yorba Linda, CA

To Lock an Adjustment

Some adjustments never seem to stay adjusted. If they rely on the clamping power of a bolt in a slot, as is often the case with radial arm saw tables, they can be locked securely

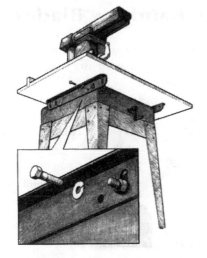

by drilling and tapping a second hole and inserting a machine screw with a lock washer. Just be sure you've got it where you want it, because the second screw allows no adjustment.

James E. Butterfield
Clarksville, TN

Sure Fire Miter Joints

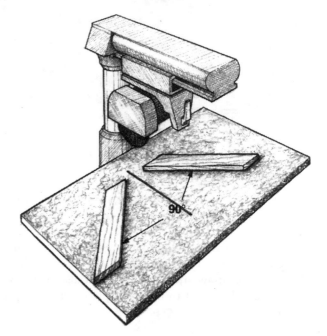

To cut accurate miters on a radial arm saw, clamp two guides on the table at 45 degrees to the blade; one right, the other left. Check them by placing a square between the two guides. A perfect miter joint will result if you saw one piece on the left guide and the mating piece on the right.

Howard K. Gaston
Holt, MI

Groovy Radial Arm Saw

Sawdust, piling up against the radial arm saw fence, can mess up the accuracy of your cuts. A groove for dust to

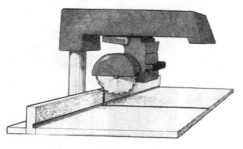

escape into can cut down the amount of brushing and blowing needed to get accurate cuts. Be sure the top of the groove is lower than the top of the thinnest stock you are likely to cut on the saw.

David Johnson
Apple Valley, MN

Sawing Plexiglas

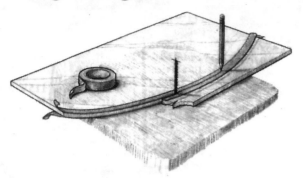

When sawing Plexiglas or similar thin plastics, I control chipping and shattering by applying masking tape to both sides of the plastic right over where the cut will go. The tape gives me a surface for marking the cut line and prevents chipping during the cut. It's been helpful with a circular saw, a bandsaw and a scroll saw. It also helps to use a fine-toothed blade and to hold the plastic sheet to prevent vibration.

Russell G. Clausing
Overland Park, KS

Keeping the Edge on Your Teeth

The spines supplied with cheap, plastic folders make great guards for handsaw blades. One spine is about right for a tenon saw or back saw; for a longer saw use two end to end.

Ben Erikson
Eutaw, AL

Erasers for Safety

When I have to cut small pieces on the bandsaw, I keep my fingers away from the blade by steering the piece with the erasers on the ends of two pencils.

Glenn Hughes
Dublin, PA

Auxiliary Bandsaw Table

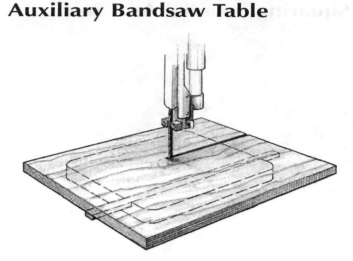

Make a wooden table to fit over your bandsaw table. Glue a strip of wood underneath to fit into the miter gauge slot (if your saw has one). This slave board, as I call it, can be aligned and clamped to the bandsaw table so that any number of jigs and fixtures can be nailed, screwed or drilled into the slave board without damaging the bandsaw table.

Bill Bigelow
Surry, NH

Brazing Bandsaw Blades

Here's a foolproof way to grind the broken ends of a bandsaw blade so the brazed joint fits together perfectly. The

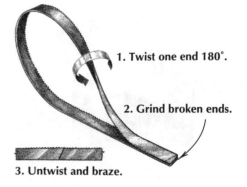

1. Twist one end 180°.

2. Grind broken ends.

3. Untwist and braze.

trick is to twist one end 180 degrees before clamping the two ends together for grinding. This way, no matter what angle you grind, you'll find that the ends fit just right when placed end-to-end for brazing.

D.F. Lucas
Jekyll Islands, GA

Resawing

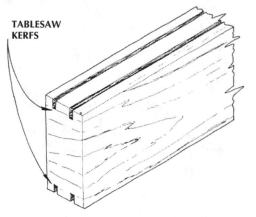

TABLESAW KERFS

Resawing is ripping a board into thinner pieces. If you find that the resawing job is putting a lot of strain on the motor of your band saw, you might still be able to accomplish the cut if you first cut guide kerfs on the table saw. These kerfs are saw cuts on the resaw line, and they reduce the amount of material the band saw blade must cut.

Jen Chiles

Resawing Narrow Stock

When resawing, most people use a fence to keep the stock perpendicular to the table. But with a fixed fence, you're in trouble if the blade has any tendency to wander. I solve the problem by resawing freehand, with my workpiece attached to one side of a 3-in. by 6-in. by 24-in. block of wood as

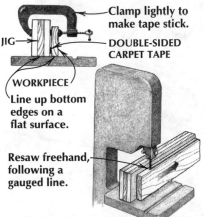

Clamp lightly to make tape stick.

JIG

DOUBLE-SIDED CARPET TAPE

WORKPIECE

Line up bottom edges on a flat surface.

Resaw freehand, following a gauged line.

shown here. This jig also allows me to cut tapers and curves—something you can't do with a fence.

E.S. Martin
Montrose, AL

A Resawing Tip

After some bad experiences with resawing a few years ago I decided to always try this simple casehardening test on my stock before resawing. Casehardening of wood refers to internal stresses which are present due to rapid drying and improper conditioning after drying. A casehardened board will look just like one which isn't casehardened. You notice the difference only when the stock is sawed or machined. If you attempt to resaw a casehardened board the wood will warp and the kerf will pinch together as you are cutting it. If you are resawing thin stock which can not be faced and surfaced to remove the warped defect the result is the production of a bunch of scrap and a wasted effort.

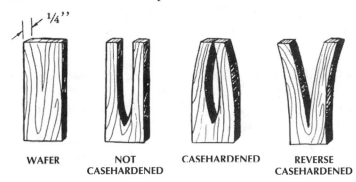

1/4"

WAFER   NOT CASEHARDENED   CASEHARDENED   REVERSE CASEHARDENED

The test for casehardening which is used by dry kiln operators is the one I use. Simply bandsaw off a cross grain, 1/4-in. thick wafer of wood approximately 6-in. in from the end of the board. Bandsaw a forked shape out of the center of the wafer. The two forked ends should remain in their original position if the board is not casehardened. If the forks pinch together or curve outward the board is casehardened and is not suitable for resawing.

Frank Pittman

Smoother Bandsaw Cuts

I rip a lot of stock into very thin pieces on my bandsaw. The blade's narrow kerf saves wood, but the teeth marks are a real problem, To lick the problem, I removed most of the set in the teeth by squeezing the blade in a pair of smooth-jaw pliers. The blade no longer cuts as tight a curve as it did, but it cuts a satin-smooth surface.

Anson Chaney
Canby, OR

To Saw A Log

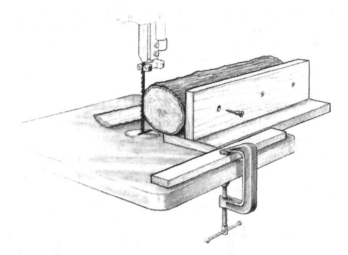

I sometimes need to saw up a small log into small boards. I screw the log to a simple T-shaped carriage to keep it under control while I saw two flat surfaces. Then I remove the carriage and use regular resawing techniques.

Ric Hanisch
Quakertown, PA

Recycling Bandsaw Blades

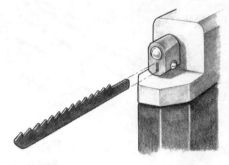

Broken bandsaw blades, if not too dull, work very well in saber saws. Snap off a piece of blade a little longer than the thickness of the stock to be cut. Grind down the teeth at one end and shape it to fit the chuck on your saber saw. Make sure the teeth are pointing up toward the chuck so the blade cuts on the pull stroke.

Howard Moody
Upper Jay, NY

Bandsaw Fence

I use my bandsaw for very accurate ripping. This fence adjusts easily by pushing in the tapered peg which locks the fence securely against the front edge of the bandsaw. A tap on the bottom of the peg releases it.

Jay Wallace
Ashland, OR

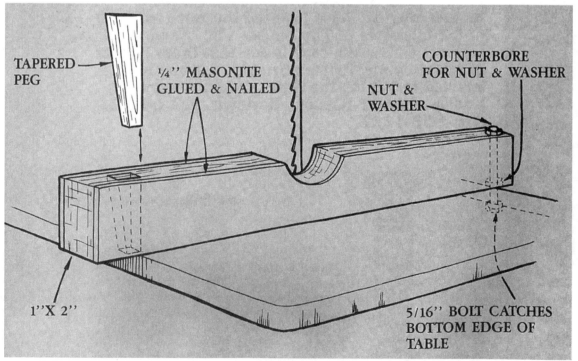

TAPERED PEG

¼" MASONITE GLUED & NAILED

COUNTERBORE FOR NUT & WASHER

NUT & WASHER

1"X 2"

5/16" BOLT CATCHES BOTTOM EDGE OF TABLE

Born-Again Brushes

Bandsaw wheels can soon get out of balance if pitch and sawdust are allowed to build up on the rubber tires. I've found that the small, bronze-bristled brushes sold to clean suede leather shoes are ideal for keeping the tires clean.

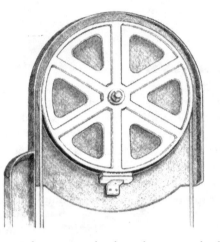

Mount one on the upper wheel, and one on the lower with steel comer brackets. You'll find that the brushes not only keep the tires free from gummy sawdust but also remove any static electricity which can cause problems in very dry climates.

Donald Kinnaman
Phoenix, AZ

Bronze Brushes Revisited

I like Donald Kinnaman's bronze brush idea, but I've found the brushes more effective when mounted on an arm that is free to move. This takes care of the brush wearing down as well as any unevenness in the wheel. A torsion or tension spring could be substituted for the weights.

Richard Quance
Almonte, Ontario

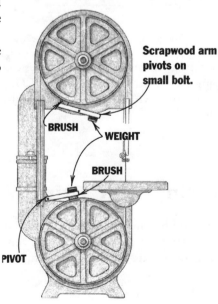

Scrapwood arm pivots on small bolt.

BRUSH

WEIGHT

BRUSH

PIVOT

Duplicate Brackets

I recently added four Victorian brackets to a screen door on my house. To save myself some time, I drew my pattern on a heavy piece of stock and then cut that design out on a band saw (Fig. 1). then resawed the piece, again on the band saw, into four brackets all exactly alike (Fig. 2).

Frank Pittman

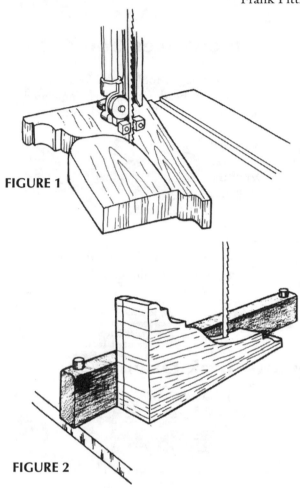

FIGURE 1

FIGURE 2

Managing Your Machinery

Taming the Power Cords

Do the cords of your power tools look like a rat's nest? Try taming them with twin-bead ponytailers. These are braided elastic hair bands with a small ball at each end. Just fold the cable in half, then in half again until you have the size you want. Wrap the ponytailer around the cord and slip the ball through the loop. Ponytailers  come in various sizes and can be found in the cosmetics department along with other hair accessories.

Charles Dilks
Richland, WA

Remote Tank Drain

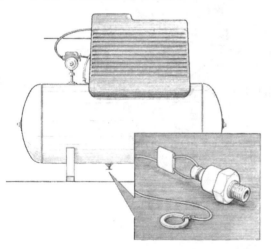

My air compressor is located conveniently out of my way, but inconveniently for draining the condensation from the tank. To solve the problem, I replaced the original drain cock with a remote tank drain valve designed for large trucks with air brakes (NAPA #66164). The new valve has a 5-ft. cable that I can pull when I need to drain the tank. When I release the cable, the valve re-closes.

Walter Colton
Wellsboro, PA

Tag That Wire

Most of my electric tools are connected to plug strips. Since all black electrical cords look alike it's hard to tell which one goes to which machine. This is not only a nuisance but could be dangerous. My solution is to wrap a colored tape around each end of the cord—at the plug and near the machine—so I can match the plug with the tool I want to use. When I run out of colors I'll use double bands of tape.

Carl Yarowski
Columbus, OH

No Fumble Toggle-Switches

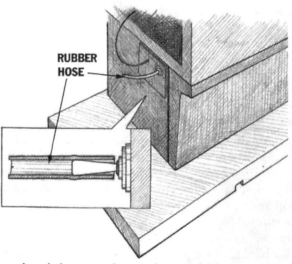

RUBBER HOSE

Recessed and short toggle switches can be improved by slipping on a short length of $1/8$-in. I.D. rubber hose. The hose makes the switch easier to find and operate without fumbling.

William Guthrie
Pontiac, MI

Losing Your Grip?

I put rubber anti-slip tape (the sort used on stair treads) on push sticks, hold-downs, and even surfaces such as the fence on a plate joiner or the clamps on a dovetail jig.

Robert G. Brandt
Fort Worth, TX

PVC Pipe Stand

I needed a stand for my grinder and bench-top disk/belt sander, but I was discouraged by the high price of manufactured stands. While at my dad's plumbing shop, the idea came to me to make a stand from 4-in. dia. PVC pipe and two toilet flanges.

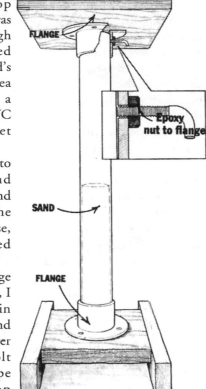

I cemented the pipe to the bottom flange and filled the pipe full of sand for ballast. I bolted the flange to a wooden base, but it could be bolted directly to the floor.

So that the top flange could swivel on the pipe, I drilled a $9/32$-in. hole in the side of the flange and epoxied a $1/4$-in. nut over the hole. A $1/4$-in. bolt bent into an "L" shape locked down the top flange on the PVC pipe.

I mounted the grinder on a piece of plywood bolted to the top flange. I painted the stand gray, and boy does it look sharp. The neat part is that I can use the same base for different tools. I just make a separate flanged base for each tool, and I can swap tools when I need to.

Bill Buhrman
Salina, KS

End Bad Vibes

To dampen machine vibrations, I drill and then countersink hockey pucks and bolt them to the feet of the machine.

Bob Vaughan
Roanoke, VA

Stop Machines

I have a small workshop, so I have to double up tools in the available space. One of my space-saving moves was to equip my workbench with four threaded insert nuts that let me easily attach or remove my scroll saw. I set them a fraction below the surface of the bench so I can install flat head machine screws to keep dust and chips from filling the holes when the scroll saw is not in use.

This idea works equally well for any bench-top machine that isn't used frequently, such as a grinder or a bench-top mortising machine.

Robert Heil
Rockford, IL

Handy Stands

I own several bench-top power tools, but I don't have the bench or floor space to set them all up at once. I devised a method to keep all my tools handy and ready to use in a matter of seconds.

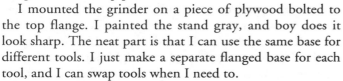

I mounted each machine on a $3/4$-in. plywood base and fastened a length of 2x4 to the bottom of each base. When I need the machine, I lay the base across the tables of my Black & Decker Workmate bench and clamp the 2x4 between the jaws. I attached an eyehook to one end of the 2x4 so I can hang the machine on the wall when not in use.

Dave Friend
Monroe, MI

Low-Tech Motor Mount

Electric motors from old washers and dryers can be useful in the shop but they often lack a base plate for mounting. Here's a way to solve the problem.

I make a base from 3/4-in. plywood, two "J" bolts and a length of perforated iron strapping. If you can't find J bolts, you can open up the loops of eyebolts.

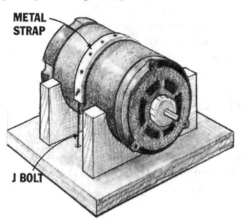

METAL STRAP

J BOLT

I find that one strap is sufficient to hold the motor in the cradle. However, you could install two straps—one at each end—if necessary to hold the motor.

Dean St. Clair
Salesville, OH

Emergency Belt

When a belt breaks, you're often in the middle of a job, so it needs replacing right away. My method is to run cotton string between the machine's two pulleys until the grooves are half full. I then tightly wrap string around this improvised belt as if I were "serving" a rope. The result is a strong, cool-running belt that takes five minutes to make. I have four of these belts now, and they've been running for well more than a year with no problems.

Michael Chilquist
Pittsburgh, PA

Dust-Collector Window

I've found that a plastic window in the side of my steel dust-collector drum is a great convenience. With a window, I can empty the drum before it gets chock-full. Cut a 2- or 3-in.-wide slot in the side of your collector drum as shown. Attach the plastic window to the outside of the drum with sheet-metal screws. A rubber gasket helps preserve the vacuum.

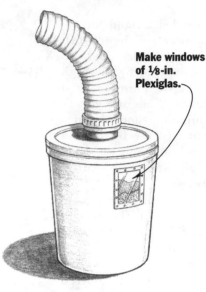

Make windows of 1/8-in. Plexiglas.

Robert McMurray
Mill Valley, CA

Double Duty Dumpsters

To make handling trash in the shop easier, I've purchased several rubber garbage cans with 5-wheel dollies. Their stability makes them suited for other uses besides handling waste. Recently, they've doubled as turntables in the spray booth while finishing. The 32-in. height makes them ideal for elevating work to be sprayed. I also use them for wheeling furniture pieces from one machine to another. The added ballast of trash makes them even less prone to tip.

Lee Maughan
Panaca, NV

Dinner-Time Signal

With machines running and ear protectors in place, it's pretty hard to get a woodworker's attention, even for dinner. An unexpected tap on the shoulder can be dangerous. I installed a light socket and red bulb at eye level, and when my wife flips the switch, I'm alerted to rejoin the rest of the world.

Scott W. Ball
San Antonio, TX

Spray Your Dust Troubles Away

When I first tried my two-bag dust collector, I noticed an unacceptable amount of fine dust escaping through the top bag. Recalling a trick I'd heard, I sprayed the inside of the upper bag with aerosol, no-stick cooking spray. This treatment stopped the finer dust with no noticeable loss of efficiency in the dust collection system.

Robert Brandt
Ft. Worth, TX

Magnetic Pick-Me-Up

Cleaning up metal shavings or sorting brass screws from brass-plated steel ones can be a chore. A magnet will pick them up, but then how do you get them off the magnet? My solution is simple and cheap. Epoxy a short length of dowel onto a round magnet (available at your local electronics store) and fit this device inside an empty film canister. When you push the magnet down, the metal particles will be attracted to it and will stick to the outside of the canister. when you raise the magnet, they'll fall off. Add a wooden ring to prevent the shavings from walking up the sides of the film canister.

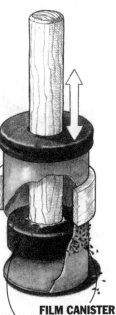

FILM CANISTER

MAGNET

Bud Moran
Riceville, TN

Self-Loading Trash Bags

I found myself knee-deep in chips and shavings after buying a shaper, but had neither the funds nor the space for a full-scale dust-collecting system. To solve the problem, I connected my shop vacuum to a plastic garbage can lined with a trash bag, and connected the garbage can to the shaper with metal dryer vent hose, as shown in the drawing.

The chips drop out in the garbage can and only the dust goes to the vacuum. The secret is to keep all the connections, including the lid, airtight. You'll have to figure out how to attach the hoses to your particular garbage can lid. Duct tape is a big help.

John O. Crenshaw
Mission Viejo, CA

Positive-Pressure Ventilation

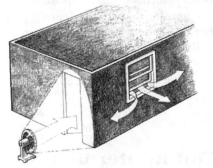

Positive-pressure ventilation (PPV) safely removes solvent fumes from a room more effectively than suction. If you place a fan 3 ft. to 12 ft. outside a room to blow through the door, the fan's cone of moving air covers the doorway and pressurizes the inside. By opening a window, you allow the pressure and fumes to escape. The room will clear quickly and no explosive fumes pass through the fan.

Steve Long
Norman, OK

Cow Magnets No Bull

This tip is for those of us with bad backs, large tummies or both. Take a broomstick and drill a 1/2-in. hole in one end. Buy a cow magnet (a cylindrical magnet with rounded ends, designed to lodge in a cow's stomach and catch nails, tin cans etc. on their way through) and epoxy

Glue magnet into end of broom handle.

it into the broom handle, leaving an inch or so exposed. With this simple tool you can retrieve metal objects, nails and small tools from the floor or behind the bench. Cow magnets are available at vet clinics and farm-supply stores.

Bear Neef
Pardeeville, WI

Router Magic

Bit-Changing Stand

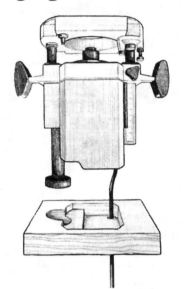

Changing router bits can be difficult, time consuming and exasperating if your router won't rest upside down on your bench. If your router has protruding handles, cords or switches, make a simple wooden jig to hold the router upside down.

Start with a scrap piece of 2x4 about 7-in. long. Drill a hole for any handle or cord, then rout out a recess to match the shape of your router body. Cord holes should be large enough so that you can drop the plug end through the hole. Clamp the jig in your bench vise to hold the router for changing bits.

Gene Payne
Sioux Falls, SD

Sticking Router Bits

A router bit seizing in the collet is a common problem, but the bit coming loose is worse because it can cause damage to the work and injury to you. I solved both these problems by coating the tapered threads on the outside of the split collet with a thin layer of oil. Since I started using the oil, I have had no problems.

If you try this, be sure not to let oil get inside the collet.

John Hertz
Lansdale, PA

Custom Router Fence

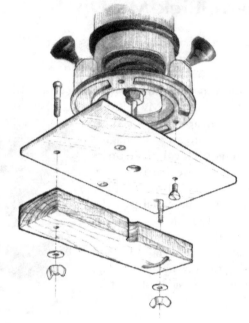

Frustrated by my inability to steadily feed wood past the bit in my router table, I took the router out of the table and combined it with this adjustable fence. The fence attaches to the base of the router and lets me control a cut while using the router freehand. The assembly has a Plexiglas base with four holes drilled for the baseplate screws and a larger one, in the center, for the bit. The fence is hardwood with a curved slot at one end, as shown, for adjusting the width of the cut. I drilled undersized holes through the Plexiglas so the two 1/4-in. bolts I used fit snugly. A couple of wing nuts with washers make the fence easily adjustable.

John McDonald
West Newbury, MA

Easy-Out Router Bits

A router bit tends to "freeze" in the collet when used a long time. The secret to freeing a bit begins when you first insert it. Push the bit all the way in, then pull it back out about 1/8 in. Now if it freezes in the collet you can tap it in with a stick of wood. The bit can break free into the 1/8-in. of room above it.

Hugh Williamson
Tucson, AZ

Router Jointing

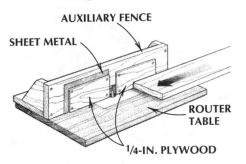

This simple jig enables you to prepare boards for edge-gluing with only a router and a regular straight bit. First make an auxiliary fence for your router table then cut two pieces of plywood. Screw them both to the fence, on either side of the bit, but slip a piece of thin sheet metal (or shirt cardboard) behind the one on the outfeed side. Adjust the fence so the cutting edge of the bit is flush with the outfeed surface of the fence. The depth of cut will be the thickness of the sheet metal. I've found this method actually produces a smoother cut than a jointer.

Kristian Eshelman
Highland Park, NJ

Router into Lamello

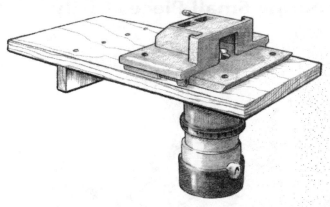

I bought the Sears Bis-Kit system to convert my router to a biscuit joiner but found it too clumsy to use with a hand-held router. So I mounted the Bis-Kit system and router to a piece of 3/4-in. oak and clamped it in a vise as a stationary machine. This gives me better control because I can use both hands to hold the work. I dedicate an extra router to biscuit joinery so I don't have to disturb the setup.

Neil Stoyanovich
Windsor, Ontario

Shaping Thin Stock

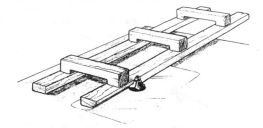

Shaping thin stock, such as picture-frame molding, on a router table can be awkward. It's easy to roll or lift the work, affecting the cut, and one's fingers are perilously close to the cutter. My solution is to attach an outrigger to the workpiece with hot-melt glue. I cut away the lower edge of the supports as shown so they'll clear the bit's pilot bearing. Then I can rout both sides of a workpiece safety.

Dale Fritz
Cypress, TX

Planing By Router

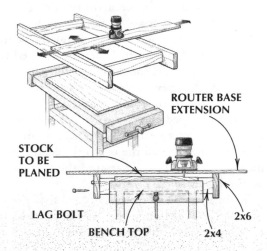

With the right jig you can do most anything with a router—even plane boards. My jig consists of a rectangular frame that guides a long auxiliary router base. I made the frame as shown, using 2x6s and 2x4s. Before assembling the frame, I jointed one edge of each 2x6, then ripped the two boards to uniform width.

I made an auxiliary router base long enough to straddle the 2x6s and enable the bit to reach anywhere within the frame. Use a stiff piece of plywood or hardwood for the base because there mustn't be any give in this piece. (Depending on the length of your bits you may have to cut a recess for the router base.)

I set the frame on my bench, clamped the 2x4s in my two tail vises, and placed the tabletop to be planed inside. Setting the router bit to just skim the surface, I went to work and planed the top flat.

Chuck LeDoux
Heppner, OR

Cutting Round Holes in Posts

While making a table base, I was confronted by the problem of cutting a round hole in the end of a large, round post. With no lathe, how was I to do this safely and accurately?

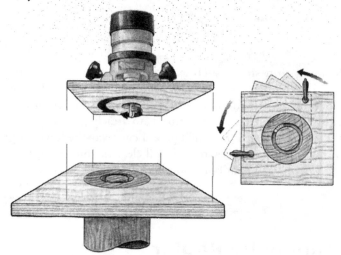

My solution was to make a router jig. First, I cut a square piece of $3/4$-in. plywood about 4 in. bigger than the diameter of the post. I placed the post at the center of the plywood and traced around it. I then bandsawed the circle, making sure the post fit snugly but could still turn in the hole. Next, I made a new baseplate for my router out of $3/8$-in. plywood and drilled a hole in the center for a $1/2$-in. straight bit. I clamped the two pieces of plywood together so the router bit was near the center. To cut the hole, I started the router, lowered the bit to the required depth-of-cut, and rotated the whole jig around the post. It cut a perfectly round hole.

The further the bit is from the center of the post, the larger the diameter of hole it cuts. If you try this, be sure to rotate the plate against the direction the router bit cuts.

Yeung Chan
Millbrae, CA

Hand-Friendly Knobs

My hand got tired of trying to tighten the small wing nut on my router, so I replaced the nut with a large plastic knob—one with a metal bushing and internal thread. If this arrangement is too cramped, you can replace the bolt with a longer one and add a bushing to take up the difference in length.

Ben Erickson
Eutaw, AL

T Square for Routing Dadoes

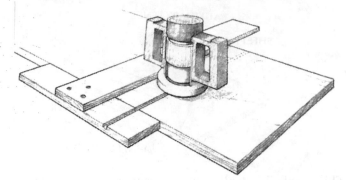

Routing dadoes is easier if you make yourself a T square long enough to cross the board. The square should overhang on each end by at least half the diameter of your router base. Clamp the square to your work with C clamps or vise grips, one at either end.

Don Taylor
Deer River; MN

Flush Trimming Pegs and Plugs

I use a router with a straight bit to flush-trim pegs and plugs. I set the bit a hair above the surface of the board and I get a consistent, clean cut that needs little or no sanding. If the pegs are spaced so closely that they interfere with the router base, I just plug and trim one at a time.

Mike Swenson
Bow, NH

Routing Small Pieces Easily

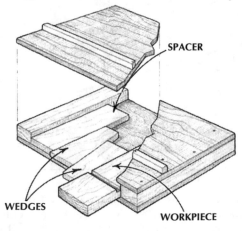

SPACER

WEDGES

WORKPIECE

When routing dadoes or moldings on the small parts of the clocks I build, I wedge them into the box-like jig shown in the drawing. The jig holds the small parts securely, and it's easy to line up the edge of the jig with a mark on the parts.

Ron Breadner
Owen Sound, Ontario

Routing Recesses for Inlays

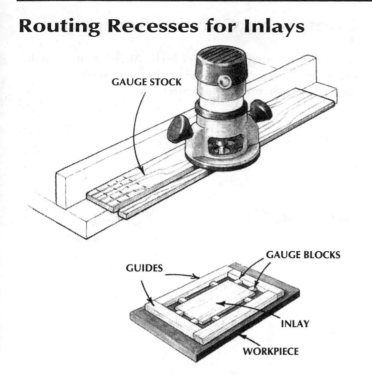

Routing a recess for an inlay is simple if you use gauge blocks to position the router guides. With a straight bit in the router, guide the base against a fence to trim a piece of stock to the proper width (the distance from the bit to the edge of the router base). Next, crosscut this gauge stock into short blocks and use them as spacers to position router guides around the inlay. Clamp the guides in place, remove the inlay and gauge blocks, and rout the recess with the same bit you used to trim the gauge stock. Square up the corners with a chisel.

Howard K. Gaston
Naples, FL

Pin Router in a Hurry

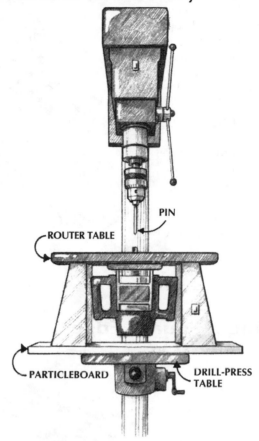

Clamp a router table to a drill-press table and you've built a pin router! Be sure the axes of the two machines line up. A steel rod or upside-down bit in the drill serves as the pin and raises or lowers with the quill.

David Jeffrey
McKinleyville, CA

Routing Flutes

To make fluted panels for columns, doors and cabinets build a sliding carriage for your router table. Make the carriage out of plywood a little over twice as long as the longest flute you intend to cut. Screw a fence to the back and clamp on stop blocks to control the beginning and end of the flute. A couple of cleats screwed to the underside of the carriage guide it along the router table and keep it from twisting. To rout a flute, put the end of the board against one stop block, lower it onto the spinning cutter and push it along the fence until it butts against the second stop block. Lift the board off the cutter and slide the carriage over to cut the next flute. This jig is really handy if you have a whole run of fluted panels to make. You only have to measure once, the jig takes care of the rest.

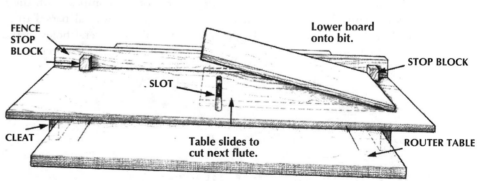

Glenn Bosroc
Carversville, PA

Rounding a Chest Top

To get the coopered top of a chest perfectly rounded, I pivot a tray for my router from the center of the arc of the chest top. The bit passes through a slot in the tray bottom and trims the chest top. The router goes from end to end of the tray while the tray pivots across the top.

Bill Voyles
Vancouver, WA

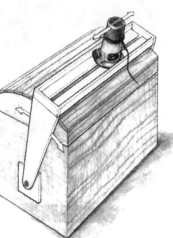

Routing a Square Edge

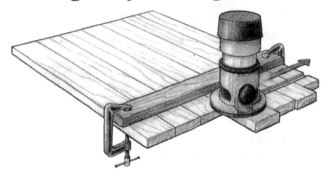

When I need to square up a panel that's too large for my tablesaw, I simply clamp a fence across the piece and trim off the excess with a 3/8-in. or 1/2-in. straight bit in my router. It takes four or five passes at increasing depths-of-cut, but the edge is unsplintered and square. This technique also works well with veneered plywood, which tends to chip out when cut with a circular saw.

Bill Kearney
Douglas, WV

Contoured Cabinet Scrapers

A router bit can clean up after itself. After I rout a moulding, I use the same bit as a miniature hand scraper to clean up burns or other minor imperfections.

Daniel C. Urbanik
Washington, PA

Routing Circles

Here's an easy way to cut perfect circles with a router. Chuck a 1/2-in. or 3/4-in, dia. straight bit in your router and screw the base of the router to a strip of 1/2-in. plywood a little wider than the router base. Switch the router on and plunge the bit through the plywood. Figure the radius of the circle you want to cut and, with the router off, measure this distance from the edge of the bit and drill a screw hole at that point. If you screw the whole plywood assembly to the piece you want to cut, you have a giant compass with the router as a cutting edge. Make the cut in several passes to avoid bogging down the router. Drilling several holes in the plywood lets you use the jig for different-size circles.

Malden Rand
Detroit, MI

Routing Large-Radius Curves

I've used this jig to rout curves with radii as small as 10-in. and as long as 14-ft. when making a curved door header. I can adjust the radius with great accuracy by loosening the clamp and sliding the pivot block in its slot.

Larry Humes
Bellingham, WA

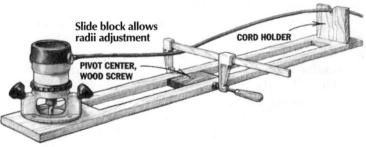

Slide block allows radii adjustment

CORD HOLDER

PIVOT CENTER, WOOD SCREW

Routing Curves Made Easy

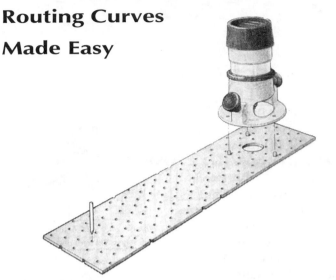

Make a simple jig to rout circles and radii. Cut a strip of Masonite Peg-Board at about a 30 degree angle to the lines of holes. Remove the router base plate, and drill holes in the Peg-Board and countersink them so you can attach the router with the same base-plate screws. Run a nail or awl through one of the Peg-Board holes to establish a pivot point. If you need some odd radius, drill an extra pivot hole to suit.

Robert Tupper
Canton, SD

Drop-In Table

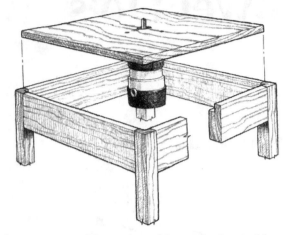

I built my router table so the tabletop fits in a rabbet along the inner edge of a frame. The weight of the router keeps the top in place, but it's removable for easy installation or adjustment of the router.

Wesley Phillips
Greer, SC

Taming The Router

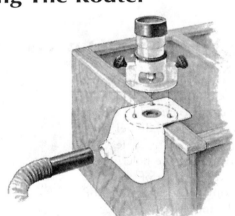

When remodeling my kitchen recently I had to rout all the face frames flush with the cabinet sides. Rather than fill the room with dust and shavings I adapted a plastic gallon milk jug to pick up the chips. I attached the milk jug to the router base plate by making a hole just big enough for the bit. Then I pushed the 1-in. hose of my shop vacuum onto the neck of the bottle, fired up the vacuum and router, and trimmed the face frames with minimal mess.

Mike Cholod
Bensalem, PA

Dado and Edge-Trimming Jig

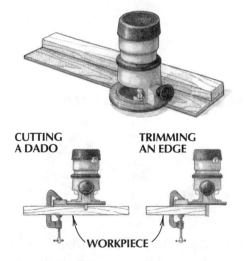

CUTTING A DADO   TRIMMING AN EDGE

WORKPIECE

With this simple jig I can use my router to trim an edge or cut a dado with great precision. I glue a straight-edged fence to a base of $1/4$-in. plywood and then trim the "working" edge of the base with a straight bit in the router. Just remember to use the same straight bit each time.

Yeung Chan
Millbrae, CA

Dowel Do's

Slotting Rods

Cutting slots safely and accurately in the ends of dowel rods can be a problem. My solution is to drill a hole the same size as the dowel in a block of wood. I then slot the block on the bandsaw so the kerf runs a few inches past the hole. A rubber band keeps the dowel firmly in the hole while I saw it. If you don't like that idea, use a small wood screw instead.

Yeung Chan
Millbrae, CA

Instant Dowel Centers

For a quick doweling job, I drive a finish nail about halfway into the wood wherever I want a dowel. I clip the head off, so only about 1/4-in. is left sticking out, and I press the mating piece firmly against the nails. Then I pull the nails and drill holes with a brad-point bit at all the points marked. Unlike when using dowel centers, you can use this technique for any size of dowel.

Martin Gross
Marlin, WA

Dealing With Dowels

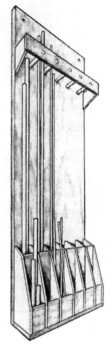

Here's a rack we've built to solve the problem of storing different lengths. Full length dowels go in the back and shorter pieces go up front. Now it's easy for us to find the diameter and length of the dowel we want.

Alice & Robert Tupper
Canton, SD

Make Your Own Dowels

The next time you need a dowel pin in some unusual hardwood, try making your own. First drill a hole the same size as the dowel in a piece of 1/4-in. steel plate, leaving the rough edges of the hole intact. Then, whittle a piece of wood to the approximate size and shape of the dowel pin. Place the plate on blocks (with the burr around the drilled hole facing up) and drive the wood through with a hammer. You can drill holes for several sizes of dowels in one plate, but you'll need to use heavier-gauge metal as the size of the dowel increases.

Danny Brumfield
LeSage, WV

V-Block for Round Stock

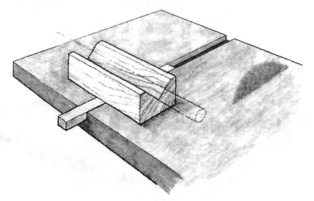

Crosscutting round stock on a bandsaw or tablesaw is easy if you make a V-block jig with a guide strip to fit the miter gauge slot in the table.

Bill Bigelow
Surry, NH

Adjustable V-Jig

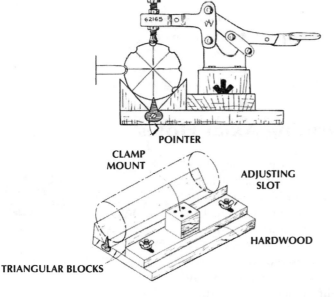

POINTER

CLAMP
MOUNT

ADJUSTING
SLOT

HARDWOOD

TRIANGULAR BLOCKS

This home-made jig is used for holding round stock while cutting in flutes or reeds down a column of wood. It may be used on a shaper or perhaps a drill press using a regular fence type set-up. Once the layout marks have been drawn on one end of the wood column, the home-made brass pointer may be adjusted to accommodate the diameter to center it up. The toggle clamps hold the wood in the position necessary. This is an easy jig to make with materials already in the shop.

Jerry Lyons

Strip O' Wheels

Faced with the task of making 80 1/2-in. dia. wheels for some toys I was making, I came up with the following idea. I drilled some 1/2-in. dia. holes in a piece of scrap wood and drove short pieces of 1/2-in. dowel into the holes. Then, I

ripped the scrap into strips the thickness of the wheels I wanted and popped the finished wheels out of the strips. This technique makes wheels without rough edges.

Lawrence L. Lucas
Mount Jackson, VA

Taming Skittish Dowels

When I'm drilling or shaping round stock, like dowels, I get a good grip and a flat reference surface by clamping the round stock in a jig like the one in the drawing. I cut the width of the groove to the diameter of the dowel. The saw kerf provides just enough "give" for the wing-nut (or screw) to clamp the jig to the dowel.

John Roccanova
Ancramdale, NY

Dowel Drilling Jig

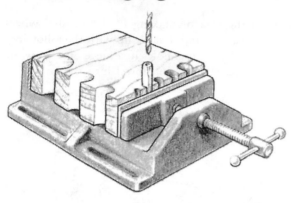

If you've ever found it frustrating to drill a hole in the end of a dowel you'll appreciate this simple jig, which fits in a machinist's vise. To make it, simply drill partial holes in a block of wood so about 1/16 in. of each dowel will be exposed when you slide it into a hole. It's best to use Forstner (rim-guided) bits, since they'll cut clean holes at the edge of the block. If Forstner bits are scarce, clamp a piece of scrap-wood to the edge of the jig and drill with a Powerbore or paddle bit. when using the jig, put a wood pad between the dowel and the steel vise jaw so the jaw doesn't mar the surface of the dowel.

Tim Green
Lancaster, CA

Simple Dowel Jig

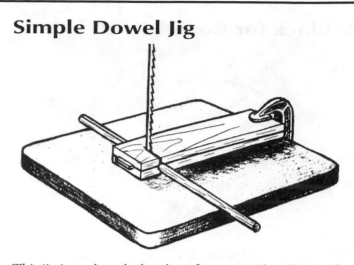

This jig is used on the bandsaw for cutting dowels in half to create half-round moulding. It consists of two pieces of wood that have a channel cut out for the dowel to fit into and a slot cut out for the blade. One end is clamped together and to the edge of the table, while the other end has a wedge insert to allow enough room for the dowel to be pushed through the jig.

Frank Pittman

Dowel-Rod Jig

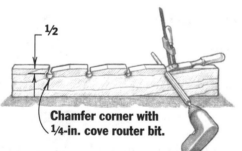

½

Chamfer corner with
¼-in. cove router bit.

This jig works very much like an old-fashioned pencil sharpener. Miter sawing and drilling in a piece of fir as shown, I clamp a 2-in.-wide chisel to it, bevel side up. The flat, on which the chisel rests, must be exactly tangent to the hole. I saw the dowel stock roughly to an octagon, chamfer one end and chuck the other end in an electric drill. Starting at slow speed, I feed the stock through the hole. Skewing the chisel slightly gives a smoother cut.

Robert Tucker
Canton, SD

Drilling Axial Holes

This is a quick, accurate method to drill axial holes in the ends of dowels or other sections too small to stand unsupported. All you need is two handscrews. Lay the handscrews on the drill-press table at approximately right angles to each other, as shown in the drawing, and tighten them around the workpiece. If you're drilling a long dowel, it can project down through the hole in the table. If the dowel is too large to fit through the hole, swing the table over to one side and let the clamps project over the edge.

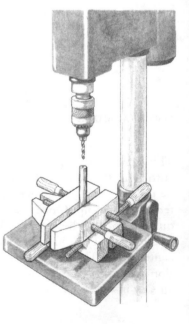

Daniel Haubert
Farmington Hills, MI

Slotting Large Dowels

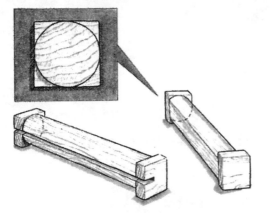

Cutting a groove in a dowel or sawing a flat on one side of it can be dangerous because the dowel has a tendency to spin. My solution is to simply glue square blocks to each end of the dowel. The length of the sides of the blocks must be the same as the diameter of the dowel (see drawing) and the two blocks must line up exactly so there is no wobble. Then you can go ahead and make your cut with perfect safety.

Yeung Chan
Millbrae, CA

Routing Large Dowels

I needed a 4-in. dia. dowel rod for a table base. I couldn't find any ready-made and didn't have a lathe to turn it myself, so I decided to rout it. First I glued up a plywood box—no top or bottom—the length of the dowel I needed. I then made a new plywood base for the router with wood strips clamped to the sides. I wanted the router to slide back and forth along the sides of the box.

With that done, I cut my 4x4 blank and drilled 3/8-in. holes at the centers of both ends. I drove 3/8-in. threaded rods into the holes to serve as a pivot. At one end, I improvised a handle.

I used a 3/8-in straight bit in the router and pushed it slowly away from me as I turned the handle. It works best to take light cuts and to saw the corners off the blank first.

Yeung Chan
Millbrae, CA

Drilling Dowels

Trying to drill a series of accurately spaced holes in a dozen pieces of dowel rod is awkward at best. My solution is to tape each rod to a straight piece of scrap so the rod can't turn, then mark the centers of the holes with pencil lines that extend across onto the scrap. To position the rod exactly under the center of the drill I put a small bit (or finish nail) in the chuck. I then clamp a fence to the drill press table and replace the bit with one of the right size.

To correctly space the holes on each succeeding rod, I just transfer the marks from the scrap. If you are drilling only one rod you can mark it directly.

Yeung Chan
Millbrae, CA

Rounding Ends of Large Dowels

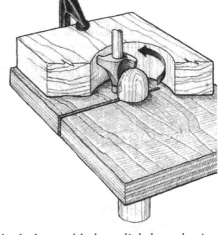

For a recent project I had to round the end of a 1 1/2-in. dia. dowel, and since I don't have a lathe I decided to use my router. First, I drilled a 1 1/2-in. hole in a piece of plywood, and sawed a slot from the edge of the plywood through to the other side of the hole. In this way, when I put the plywood in a vise the hole would close slightly and grip the dowel. Next, I made a support plate for the router and drilled a 4-in. hole in the middle with a fly-cutter.

I then mounted a carbide tipped round-over bit in my router. The bit was fitted with a pilot bearing the same radius as the rod —3/4 in. With the dowel locked in the plywood and the support plate clamped on top, I rounded the dowel in three or four passes, lowering the router bit a fraction each time, and moving it always against the direction of cut.

Yeung Chan
Millbrae, CA

Drill Press Pointers

Keeping Holes in Line

It can be difficult to drill a deep hole and have the bit exit where expected. My solution is to turn a wood insert to fit the hole in my drill-press table. In the exact center of this insert I place a nail with the point sticking up about 1/4-in. Then I chuck a brad-pointed bit of the size I want and swing the table so the point of the nail and the tip of the bit are in line. I mark the centers of the work at both ends and 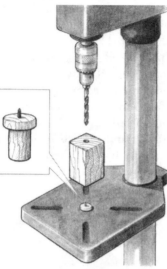 then drill the hole with the drill press. I stop just short of the nail and finish drilling the hole at the bench.

Ron Pavelka
Orange, CA

Getting the Right Angle

This jig is handy for drilling perpendicular holes without being limited by the throat of your drill press. Use hardwood—or metal if the jig will be used often—but bore all the initial holes on a drill press to make sure they are square to the base. I made my jig to accommodate drill sizes from 1/16 in. to 1/2 in.; you can modify that for your needs. Be sure to hold the jig firmly when drilling or, better still, clamp it.

Boles Derenda
West Seneca, NY

Drilling Jig Guide

When drilling holes in a piece of wood longer than the drill bit length but not twice that distance, you may set-up an operation similar to the sketch shown. Drill half-way through on all pieces and then set-up a guide pin and drill from the opposite end to line up exactly with the first hole drilled.

Jerry Lyons

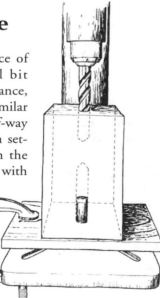

Hole in One

To drill holes exactly centered on a sphere, I first clamp a piece of scrap to the drill-press table. Then I drill a hole with a diameter about three quarters that of the sphere. Without disturbing the setup I change bits, position the ball in the hole, hold it firmly and drill. I used this trick when drilling the feet for the napkin holder featured in AW #38.

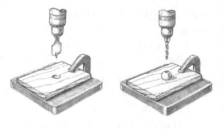

Yeung Chan
Millbrae, CA

Dowel Depth Stop

A quick depth stop can be made from a piece of dowel. Drill a hole through the length of a dowel and slide the dowel until it meets the chuck. The length of bit protruding in front of the dowel equals the depth of the holes to be drilled.

Christian Becksvoort

Quick-Step Depth Stop

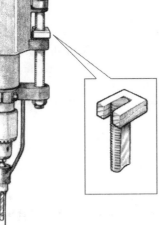

This is a useful gadget for anyone cutting haunched mortises on the drill press with a hollow chisel mortiser. Make a U-shaped wood block that fits loosely around the depth stop rod as shown. After cutting the deep mortise, slip the block around the stop rod and then cut the shallower, haunched part.

Ben Erickson
Eutaw, AL

More on Homemade Drill Bits

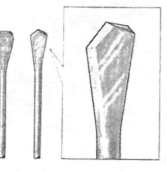

H.R. McDermid's Tech Tip on homemade drill bits reminds me of an old boat builder I used to work with, Jim Smith. Jim kept a roll of heavy galvanized fence wire in his shop. Whenever he needed a fresh bit for his drill he would cut off about a 4-in. length of wire, straighten it and then flatten one end on an anvil. (See drawing.) His final step was to grind the end to a diamond-shaped point on a bench grinder. These homemade drills didn't last forever, but it was only a two minute job to replace one. I've found that heavy-gauge coat hangers work equally well.

Pat Jordan
San Francisco, CA

Low-Tech Depth Stop

When drilling holes, I use tape for a depth stop. It never slips. Wrap the tape around the bit with an extra inch sticking out. As you near your desired depth, this wing of tape will begin sweeping away the wood chips around the hole. When all the chips are swept away, you've reached your desired depth.

Aaron Black
Simpsonville, SC

Blow the Chips Away

I make a lot of cribbage boards. Often, the wood chips from the drill press obscure the marks I've made for the adjoining holes. To eliminate the problem, I mount a small, wooden propeller on the drill bit, which blows the chips away.

I shape the propeller with a belt sander and then drill through it at a slow speed, leaving it on the bit a 1/4 in. above your work when the bit is all the way down.

Dale Jennings
Littlefork, MN

Penny-a-Piece Drill Bits

Tired of replacing the smaller sizes of bits? I've stopped altogether and now clip the heads off finish nails and use them instead of drills. The smooth nails—not galvanized seem to work best. I use these improvised bits for drilling pilot holes because the exact size of the hole doesn't matter. They'll cut even better if you file or grind the end of the nail to a chisel point.

H.R. McDermid
Vernon, B.C., Canada

Drilling on the Mark

Sometimes I need to drill a hole through an irregularly shaped piece and have the hole enter and exit at exactly the right spots. I made a simple jig for my drill press that makes this task easy.

I filed a point on a piece of threaded rod and cut two large washers out of thin plate steel. To drill the hole, I bolt the threaded rod through my drill press table and carefully align the drill point over the pointed end of the rod. I then center-punch the work at the desired hole entrance and exit points. I place the exit mark on the point of the rod and line up the entrance mark with the drill. To prevent tear-out, I drill approximately 3/4 of the way through, then flip the piece upside down, placing the hole over the pointed rod. I align the drill with the exit mark and finish drilling the hole from this side.

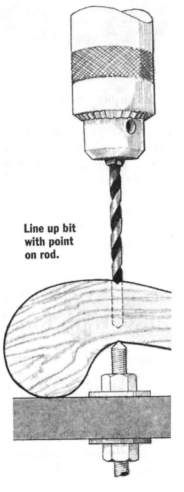

Line up bit with point on rod.

Ralph Aument
Selinsgrove, PA

Spinning Your Wheels

When making wheels for toys, I cut the blanks with a hole saw, which leaves the outside edges rough. To sand them I choose a dowel that's slightly larger than the hole in the wheel, then chuck one end in the drill press, and taper the other end with a wood file or coarse sandpaper. Then I push a wheel up the taper until it grabs, and I sand the edge while it is spinning. The larger the wheel, the slower you should run the drill press.

Ron Pavelka
Orange, CA

Boring Jig

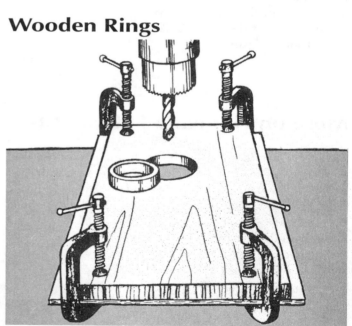

This is a neat little jig to make when you have a series of holes that all need to be drilled at the same angle. Any angle can be chosen, just be sure and align the center and side lines of the jig with the center lines of the holes to be drilled in the project.

Frank Pittman

Wooden Rings

Next time you get the urge to make wooden rings, try this method. Clamp the wood from which you plan to make the rings to a sheet of waste board. Drill a smaller hole with a hole-saw blade. Now replace the blade with a large one and without moving anything, re-center the drill and cut the outer ring. You now have a wooden ring, ready to be sanded and finished.

Frank Pittman

Drilling Pocket Holes

This simple jig prevents bits from "walking" when you're drilling pocket holes. First I find the approximate drilling angle—say 15deg.—and double it to get 30. I then cut a scrap of wood to this angle and clamp it to the workpiece, placing the vertex where I want the drill to enter. Then I drill the hole, bisecting the 30 angle by eye.

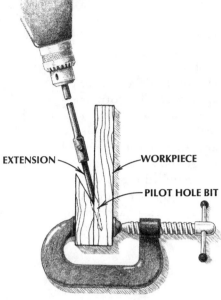

EXTENSION

WORKPIECE

PILOT HOLE BIT

The jig is sacrificial, but it's usually good for several holes. It helps to use wood of similar hardness to the stock.

Glenn Sadler
Myrtle Beach, SC

Drilling Compound Angles

I use this jig frequently when making chairs. Designed to be used on the drill press, it makes accurate work of boring holes at compound angles. I made the jig with three pieces of 3/4-in.-thick maple, hinging the pieces on adjacent edges as shown. I cut each one about an inch larger than the drill press table and then glued ledger strips around the perimeter of the bottom one. This keeps the jig firmly in place.

To adjust the angle I got a pair of sliding lid supports. For heavier duty applications you could use the hardware made for awning windows. By drilling a hole down

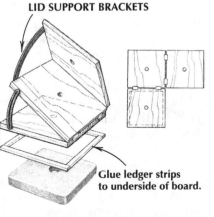

LID SUPPORT BRACKETS

Glue ledger strips to underside of board.

through all three pieces to match the one in the cast iron table, the jig can be left permanently installed.

Anthony Machiavelli
Thomaston, ME

Countersinking in Tight Corners

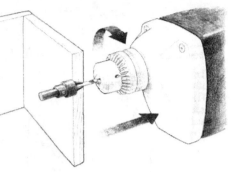

To countersink for screws on drawer knobs or handles, I first drill the shank hole from the outside of the drawer. Next, I push the drill part of a combination countersink through the hole from the inside, chuck the bit in the drill from the outside, switch the drill to reverse, and pull the rotating countersink to the correct depth.

Paul Wagstaff
Flemington, NJ

No-slip Countersink Drills

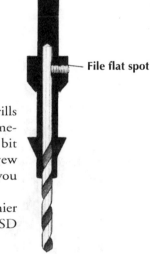

File flat spot

The drill bit on countersink drills often slips in the collar. To remedy this, file a flat spot on the bit in the area where the set-screw grabs. The bit will stay where you want it.

Kevin J. Pammier
Sioux Fails, SD

Boring the Odd Hole

I often need to drill odd-sized holes for which I don't have a standard bit. So, I make my own from spade bits. For example, recently I wanted a hole to fit 1/2-in. electrical conduit. Since the pipe was a fraction over 11/16 in., I started with a 3/4-in. spade bit and ground a fraction off each edge. I was careful to keep the bit symmetrical, cooling the steel frequently with water. As I got closer to the size I wanted, I chucked the bit and drilled trial holes until I had the correct diameter. The final step was to remove the burr by honing the bit flat on an oilstone.

John Matthews
Champaign, IL

Bit of a New Twist

You can just about eliminate tearout when drilling through holes in wood by regrinding the tip of a regular twist bit.

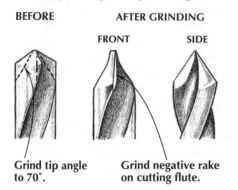

BEFORE

AFTER GRINDING

FRONT

SIDE

Grind tip angle to 70°.

Grind negative rake on cutting flute.

These modified bits are especially useful when you can't use a backing block—as when drilling through round stretchers or legs, for example. I found it essential to grind flats on the inside, as shown, so the cutting action comes close to that of a scraper. Omit this step and the bit is liable to grab.

Bill McCarthy
Riegelsville, PA

Freehand Pocket Screw Holes

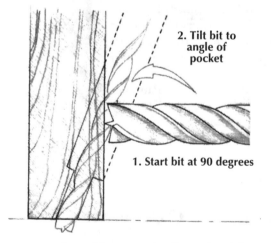

2. Tilt bit to angle of pocket

1. Start bit at 90 degrees

One way to attach a table top to its frame is with screws in pocket holes angled up through the apron. I drill these holes with a hand drill and a $1/2$ in. brad-point drill bit. I start drilling about 1 to $1 1/4$ in. from the edge of the apron with the drill at 90 degrees to the surface of the board. When the hole has been scored on the board, I start tipping the drill upward until it is at the desired angle for the pocket. Once I've drilled the counterbore for the screw head, I switch to a smaller bit and complete the hole through to the edge of the board.

Henry W. Rodgers
Dansville, NY

Turned Balls on the Drill Press

I needed to make a $1 1/2$-in.-dia. ball with a hole in it. I started with a $1 9/16$-in. cube, then scribed $1 1/2$-in.-dia. circles on all faces. After sawing off the corners with a handsaw, I drilled a tapered hole and inserted a $1/4$-in. hanger bolt. I then chucked the free end in the drill press and rounded the block with a rasp and files, finishing with fine sandpaper. Finally, I removed the hanger bolt and drilled a hole of appropriate size for the project.

Yeung Chan
Millbrae, CA

Quill Lock-Up

when you're positioning work under the bit on your drill press, it's handy to clamp the quill—this keeps it from retracting when you let go of the spoke. But many machines lack this useful feature, so here's how to add it to your drill press.

Find the threaded bolt or setscrew that engages with a keyway cut in the side of the quill to prevent it from turning. Replace this assembly (slack the lock nut first), then find a bolt or machine screw with an identical thread, but a couple of inches longer. Grind down the end to match the original bolt, then make a wooden knob and fasten it with two nuts as shown. When screwed into the hole, this assembly will lock the quill in any position. Back it off a fraction of a turn and it will still engage the keyway while allowing the quill to move freely.

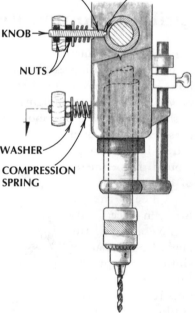

Grind end of threaded rod to match keyway.

SLOTTED KEYWAY

KNOB

NUTS

WASHER

COMPRESSION SPRING

A compression spring under the knob will provide enough friction to keep it from wandering.

Tim Hanson
Indianapolis, IN

Auxiliary Drill-Press Table

This removable auxiliary table clamps to the support column of a drill press and catches most of the waste, keeping the shop tidier and saving cleanup time. It's also a handy place to put the chuck key, spare bits, and drill-press accessories. A bonus is that it catches mortising chisels, Forstner bits, and other easily damaged drills that could fall through the hole in the metal table and strike the pedestal or floor.

I made my table from 3/4-in. plywood faced with Formica. The slick surface of the laminate makes oil and metal cleanup easy. The supporting bracket is a piece of 16-in. long 2x6 fir, which is attached to the table with wood screws. The bracket is clamped to the column with a 3/8-in. bolt, as shown.

Kenneth Broun
Virginia Beach, VA

Taming the Drill Press

I've never had any trouble lowering the table on my drill press, but I'm going on 80 now and raising it without a crank is getting harder. My solution is to attach a simple tackle to the collar as shown. To raise the table, I slack the

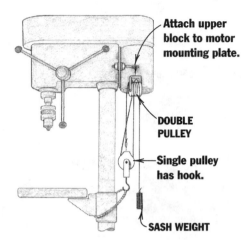

Attach upper block to motor mounting plate.

DOUBLE PULLEY

Single pulley has hook.

SASH WEIGHT

clamp and pull down on the line. The iron sash weight keeps tension in the line and also acts as a counterbalance. You can get the pulleys and 5/16-in. nylon line at your local hardware store.

Oscar Williams
Lincoln, NE

Drilling Holes in Glass

Wine bottles make handsome lamp bases, if you can drill a hole through the glass for the electrical cord. My trick is to fill the bottle with water, cork it, and cradle it in a sandbag set on my drill press table. Then I drill with a carbide-tipped cement drill bit. (500 rpm is about the right speed.) The water dissipates the heat so the glass won't crack.

To drill a hole in sheet glass, use a putty dam to retain the water, or put the glass in a shallow tray with a piece of plywood underneath as backing.

Donald Kinnaman
Phoenix, AR

Drill-Press Paper Punch

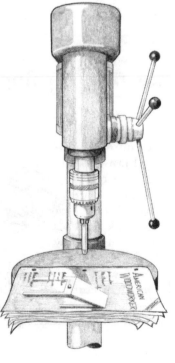

I like to store my back issues of AMERICAN WOOD-WORKER for future reference. Three-ring binders are the best way to do this, but AW does not arrive pre-punched, and it's tough to get through 80 pages. My solution is a 3/8-in. hollow punch made to punch holes in leather (available from Tandy Leather outlets). I hone the cutting edge sharp and smooth, then chuck the punch in the drill press with a piece of hardwood scrap underneath. It cuts perfectly.

Truett Frazier
Sevierville, TN

Turning Tricks

High Class Furniture Levelers

Elegant leveling feet can be an integral part of your furniture design. Epoxy a carriage bolt into a turning blank, then spin it into the screw chuck shown to turn it to suit your taste. A threaded insert in the bottom of the furniture leg completes the arrangement.

Gordon Krupp
Northbrook, IL

Kerfing Turning Blanks

Most turners cut two saw kerfs in the end of a turning blank so the spurs on the drive center can get a better bite. I rest the blank on a V-block and saw these kerfs on the bandsaw. This is safer than cutting freehand and guarantees that the kerfs run from corner to corner.

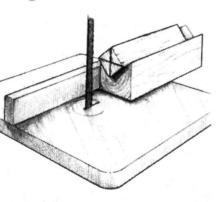

Bill Bigelow
Surry, NH

Shop-Made Lathe Gauge

I make Windsor chairs and needed a quick way to check the diameters of legs and stretchers while the parts were still on the lathe. So, I made a half-template. I drew the necessary

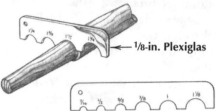

1/8-in. Plexiglas

Size half-circles
for frequently used dimensions.

profiles full-size on paper, then I folded the paper in half, tore it along the line and used spray adhesive to stick this half-pattern to 1/8 in. Plexiglas. (Plexiglas is thin enough to fit in the slot made by a parting tool.) I cut out the half-circles on a scroll saw and smoothed the edges with a spindle sander.

Sean Landers
Ayer, MA

Tenon Sizing Gauge

Here's a sizing gauge for lathe-turned tenons that's faster than measuring with calipers.

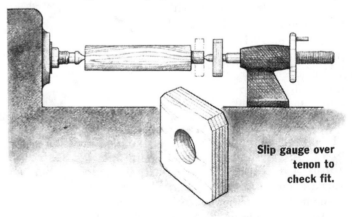

Slip gauge over
tenon to
check fit.

Drill a hole in a piece of scrap plywood with the same bit you'll use for the mortis hole. Cut the corners off the scrap and slip it over the tail-stock center. To check the fit, slip the gauge over the tenon as you turn.

Jeff Day
Perkasie, PA

Turning Toy Tires

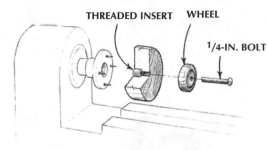

THREADED INSERT   WHEEL

1/4-IN. BOLT

If you make many toys with wheels, you'll appreciate my mandrel for turning wheels on the lathe. I rough cut the wheels with a $1/4$-in. pilot bit on a hole saw. A $1/4$-in. bolt screws into a threaded insert to secure the wheels quickly and easily for turning.

Gordon E. Krupp
Northbrook, IL

Spinning Your Wheels

My wife's current condition has awakened a heretofore dormant interest in making toys. Now we're talking about toys for MY BABY, not mass production, so I want to make everything myself. That doesn't mean, however, that I want to take all day. Here's a method I use for turning toy wheels quickly by reducing the time required for mounting them on the lathe. Turn a short spindle to hold the wheel blank onto a block mounted on a faceplate. Put the wheel on the spindle, slip it into the faceplate block, and tighten the tail stock. As a fair amount of pressure is required, a ball bearing center is helpful. The spindle is small enough to let you turn the face of the wheel. If the block is smaller than the

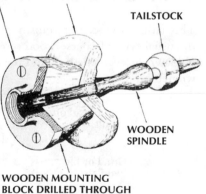

FACE PLATE OF LATHE   WHEEL

TAILSTOCK

WOODEN SPINDLE

WOODEN MOUNTING BLOCK DRILLED THROUGH

wheel blank, both edges can be rounded without reversing the wheel. A bowl gouge (this is faceplate work) ground to either a thumbnail or superflute shape should be able to shape the wheel face and round the edges without moving the tool rest. If, however, you MUST scrape, an "L" shaped tool rest made of $1^1/2$-in. laminated plywood and a dowel post would save some time—you'd only have to move it to mount the next wheel.

David R. Smith
Baltimore, MD

Center Locator

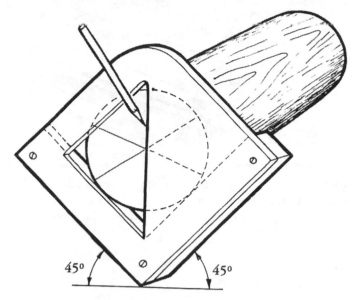

45°   45°

This tool is handy for finding the exact center of a piece of round stock. To use, rotate the round object and draw lines. Where the lines intersect is the center point of the stock. The front is Plexiglas and the back is Plexiglas or hard wood. The two are fused together with solvent if using Plexiglas or flathead wood screws if using a wood backing. It is important to make sure that all corners are exactly 90 deg. This center locator can be made any size.

Jay Wallace
Ashland, OR

Lathe Suction

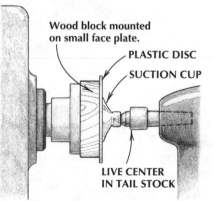

Wood block mounted on small face plate.

PLASTIC DISC

SUCTION CUP

LIVE CENTER IN TAIL STOCK

I needed to cut two clear plastic discs with smooth edges for a kaleidoscope. (See AW #40.) I cut them roughly to shape and then mounted them on the lathe using a small suction cup, as shown. Taking very light cuts with a sharp skew chisel, I found I could quickly turn a disc with a smooth, finished edge.

William Boyd
Bloomfield Hills, MI

Long Holes

PLUG

Long parts requiring a hole through the inside may be grooved, glued together and plugged at both ends so it may be placed in a lathe or for other purposes. The groove may be cut on a table saw.

Jerry Lyons

Whipping Whip on the Lathe

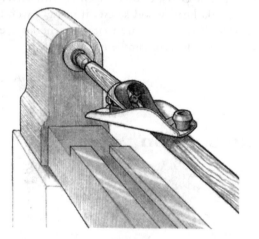

Long, thin spindles that whip and chatter on the lathe can be tamed with a steadyrest, but then you have to move the steadyrest to turn the center section. When I'm turning straight, tapered or slightly curved surfaces, I find that they whip and chatter much less if I use a hand plane instead of a skew chisel.

After roughing out the spindle with a gouge, I set the lathe speed as low as possible and "plane" the spindle with slow, even strokes. Experiment with blade settings, the angle of the plane to the spindle, the speed of your stroke, and lathe speed for the results you want.

If you're still getting some chatter, try bearing down slightly on the plane or supporting the spindle from behind with your hand.

Fred Matlack
Emmaus, PA

Lathe Tray

Woodturning produces a considerable amount of waste shavings and chips, causing things you put on the lathe bed to disappear. A plywood tray at the right-hand end of the lathe bed will hold calipers, gauges and tools away from most of the clutter.

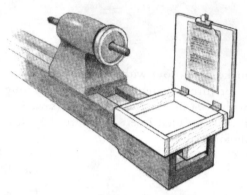

How the tray is attached to the bed depends on the design of the lathe, but it should be removable in the event you need to move the tailstock to the far end of the bed.

A refinement is a plywood lid, hinged at the back. If you arrange the hinges so the lid tilts back slightly when open, it becomes a place to clip drawings or notes so you can see them while turning.

Percy Blandford
Stratford-upon-Avon, England

Your Own Screw-Drive Center

This lathe drive center transmits torque much better than the usual type of coarse wood screw. To make one, find an old lawn-mower axle bolt and file two flats so you can slip a wrench on it.

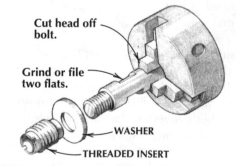

Cut head off bolt.

Grind or file two flats.

WASHER

THREADED INSERT

Put a washer over the end of the bolt, coat the threads with epoxy and screw on a 3/8-in. threaded insert. Then drill a 1/2-in.-deep hole in the center of your turning blank and screw the threaded insert into it. Put the shank of the bolt in your lathe chuck and you're in business.

Lyle Terrell
New Orleans, LA

Painting Grooves

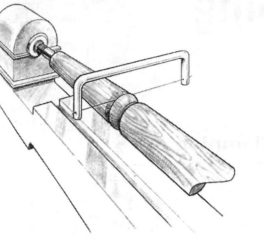

I use this simple device to accent grooves of spindle turnings with gold or silver paint. I saturate the string with spray paint and touch the string to the groove as the work turns slowly on the lathe.

A.J. Tryba
Benton, IL

Charring Decorative Lines

Decorative lines cut into tool handles and similar turned objects are often made more prominent by charring the tool-cut lines with a length of iron or steel wire held against the revolving wood. Pressure on the wood soon builds up enough friction and heat to char a good, black line, but the wire also gets too hot to hold.

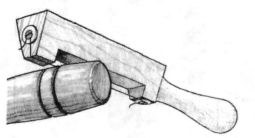

I've made a tool that enables me to do a more efficient job and avoid burning myself. The tool holds a 6-in. length of 18-gauge wire. So the wire can be tensioned or replaced, I twist its ends around screws with washers under their heads to prevent slipping.

Percy Blandford
Stratford-upon-Avon, England

Matching Half-Round Turnings

I make matching half-round turnings for the restoration of antique clock cases. I use contact cement to glue two blanks together, back to back. After turning, I start prying the two pieces apart with a chisel, dribbling a little lacquer thinner in the resulting crack. As it grows, I add more thinner until the two halves pop apart. The two turnings are a full half-round with no loss to a saw kerf.

David Johnson
Apple Valley, MN

Filing Tool Rests

File the top edge of your lathe tool rest occasionally to remove any nicks. Nicks on the tool rest hinder smooth movement of the tools.

Bill Bigelow
Surry, NH

Putting Backbone in Your Lathe

The best way to stiffen up a wood lathe—the type with hollow, tubular beds—is to fill the pipes with cement. Pop off the pipes' end caps, mix up some sand/cement mix (Sakcrete or the equivalent), and fill both pipes. Let it cure for a couple of weeks, then replace the caps. You'll be amazed how this treatment reduces vibration.

Michael Chilquist
Pittsburgh, PA

Gluing and Clamping

Ripping Stock for Glue-Up

When ripping stock for edge gluing, try alternating the boards face side up and face side down. You'll find that even if the blade is not set at exactly 90 degrees to the saw table, the slight error cancels and the glued-up panel will be perfectly flat.

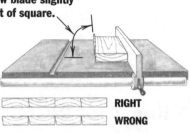

Saw blade slightly out of square.

RIGHT

WRONG

Howard Gaston
Naples, FL

Clamping Aid

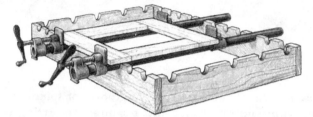

I keep my pipe clamps level, parallel, and properly spaced for glue-ups by arranging them in notches in a frame, as shown. By cutting the notches 3/4 in. deep, the upper surface of the pipes remain above the surface of the notched frame.

Mark McClain
Rawlins, WY

Non-Stick Clamping

When gluing up a project, place a piece of old-fashioned wax paper between the work and each clamp or clamping block. This keeps glue from sticking the project to the clamp or blocks.

Walter J. Morrison
Northport, NY

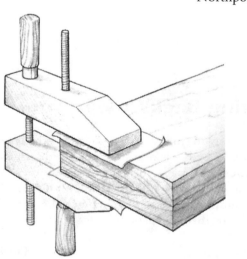

Caulk Counter Bowing

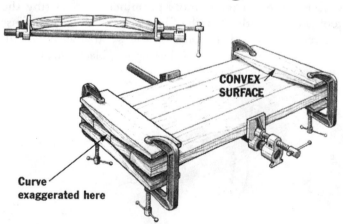

CONVEX SURFACE

Curve exaggerated here

Pressure from clamps can make a wide glued-up panel bow. Slightly convex battens top and bottom counter this pressure. Giving the cauls a coat of paste wax will keep the glue from sticking.

Jeff Day
Perkasie, PA

Wooden Wedge Clamp

If you're like me, there never seems to be enough clamps during assembly of a piece of furniture.

Here's a device I often use when boards have to be joined edge to edge or tenons pulled tight in a flat frame. Two long 1-in. by 2-in. strips are firmly fixed at one end to each side of a 2-in. block. At the other end, I've drilled holes to take a 1/2-in. bolt.

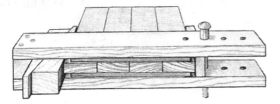

In use, the assembly goes over the job, then a flat piece of wood goes against the bolt to prevent marking the wood. Two opposing, identical wedges with slopes about 1 in 6, hammered opposite ways, exert as much force as any screw clamp. An added bonus of this device is that you can keep the glued boards flat by inserting spacers under the strips—something you can't do with an ordinary bar clamp.

Percy Blandford
Stratford-upon-Avon, England

Clamping Curved Edges

Pipe clamps tend to slip on curved edges. Here's a device I made from a 1x2 that allows me to clamp curved edges. I use it mostly for repairing tabletops, but it also can be used to glue up boards that have one straight edge and one curved edge.

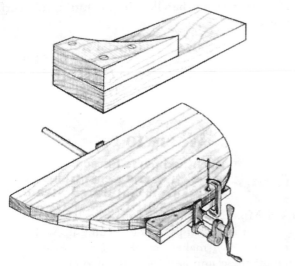

I clamp the device to the curved edge with a C clamp to hold it in place. Now the pipe clamp can be installed to clamp the boards together.

Kenneth T. May
Jeanerette, LA

Gluing Circular Segments

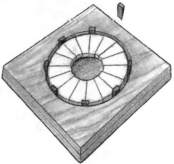

I cut a circle in a piece of 3/4-in. plywood to make a jig for gluing segments of a circle together for rings or frames. The diameter of the hole should be about 1/8 in. to 3/16 in. larger than the diameter of the circular segments.

Clamp the plywood jig on a piece of 3/4-in. plywood with wax paper in between to keep the segments from sticking to the plywood underneath.

Assemble the segments inside the circle, then push or drive small wooden wedges between the jig and the segments. The wedges push each segment toward the center and close up the gaps between segments.

C.E. Rannefeld
Decatur, AL

Flossing the Cracks

A good way to work glue into a crack or split is with unwaxed dental floss. Make a little pool of glue on the upper surface, then pull the floss (and glue) gently down through the crack.

Deanna Driscoll
San Francisco, CA

Frame Clamp

When I was a kid, my dad had a clever rig for gluing up picture frames—one that I still use. He cut L-shaped corner blocks out of 2x4s and grooved the backs to take a 1-in. web or strap clamp. To make your own, remember to round the sharp corners of the grooves so the strap will slide easily around them. Be sure to cut the inside corners of the blocks at exactly 90 degrees, so the frame will square itself as you tighten the band.

BAND CLAMP

WOOD CORNER BLOCKS

Ralph Street
Houston, TX

Pipe-clamp Jaw Protectors

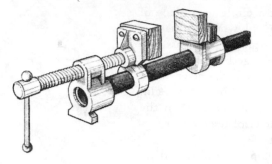

To make pipe clamps a little more manageable and to keep the steel jaws from damaging the edges of your project, fasten small softwood blocks to the jaws. This eliminates the need for that "third hand" to hold a protective scrap of wood in place while adjusting the clamps.

Simply drill two holes through each steel jaw and fasten the blocks with several pan-head screws.

Don Scarbury
Albuquerque, NM

Styrofoam Clamp Pads

When laminating curved surfaces, I use 1-in. or 2-in. thick Styrofoam as clamp pads. The pads form to the radius of the curved surface, resulting in even clamp pressure.

Brian J. O'Connor
Wolverine, MI

Deluxe Clamp Pads

When clamping up finished surfaces with iron clamps, you need wood pads—fast. My pads stay put in any position yet are easily removed by pulling out the wood pin. The bearing surfaces are

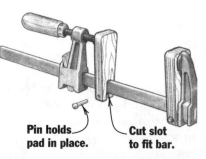

Pin holds pad in place.

Cut slot to fit bar.

larger than those on the metal pads, so they're less likely to dent the wood. Plywood faced with a soft wood such as poplar or pine works best, but fir would do.

I made several sets of pads, both for my regular bar clamps and for my miniature clamps. I used 7/32-in. wood axle pegs for the pins, but 1/8-in. cotter pins would work equally well.

Ralph Sanders
Shoreham, NY

Padding the Clamps

I used to hunt around for scraps of wood to protect my projects from iron clamps. Then I tried cutting out pieces of green felt to match the clamp pads and attaching them with double-sided tape. Now I've switched to pressure sensitive Velcro, which works even better. I cut the Velcro to size, strip off the backing and apply it to the clamp pads.

Mike Paliotta
Horseheads, NY

Padding the Clamps: Yet Another Solution

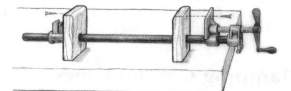

I don't need to hunt around the shop for scrapwood clamp pads, because I attach wooden pads directly to the clamps. I make my pads out of ash, round the inside corners and run a screw through the iron and into the wood. The pads are tall enough so the clamp sits conveniently upright, and you can turn the clamp handle without hitting the surface of the bench.

Art Trent
Calgary, Alberta

Clamp-Padding Take 2

I liked Mike Paliotta's idea of using felt pads to protect wood from iron clamps, but I've come up with something better: leather. I make a cardboard pattern by tracing the shape off the clamp and then use it to cut pads out of the tongues of old shoes. For removable pads, use rubber cement or double-sided tape. Otherwise glue the leather to the iron surface with Titebond glue or the equivalent.

Allison Cleary
Huntington, VT

No-Slip Clamp

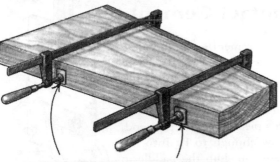

DOUBLE-SIDED FOAM ADHESIVE TAPE

When I use my bar clamps at an angle, I prevent the clamps from slipping with foam tape that has adhesive on both sides. It helps protect the wood, too. If necessary, a little naptha removes leftover tape.

M. Scally
Albuquerque, NM

To Cap It All

Glue bottle caps are mighty elusive—on the bench one minute, gone the next. I now keep a stock of the conical plastic caps sold as "wire nuts" in the electrical supply section at hardware stores and home centers. Just pull the wire spiral out and you're in business. Incidentally, plastic mustard containers make excellent glue bottles.

Will Foxx
Little Rock, AR

Pipe Clamp Pack

Gluing up can be a pleasant experience, or a nightmare. Clamp arrangement and planning ahead can mean the difference between success and failure. I've developed a sawhorse type clamp rack that holds 3/4-in. pipe clamps upright and at equal spacing during glue ups. To make the tops of the racks, I edge-glue two 5-ft. lengths of 2x6, then drill equally spaced, 1-in. dia. holes down the center. Then I rip the piece down the middle.

Lee Maughan
Panaca, NV

Model Maker's Clamp

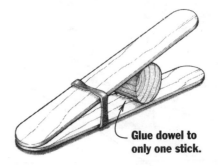

Glue dowel to only one stick.

This light-duty clamp is ideal for model makers. All you need are some 5-in. wooden tongue depressors or popsicle sticks, a rubber band, and a piece of dowel rod. You can vary the pressure by changing where you place the rubber band and how many times you wrap it around the sticks.

Jim Tite
Fayetteville, AR

Thinning Glue

I recently wrote to the Borden company, asking what to do when their Elmer's Professional Carpenter's Wood Glue gets too thick to use. They suggested mixing in a drop or two of vinegar. It sounded like a "home remedy" but I tried it and found it really works.

Lewis Michener
Solebury, PA

Jiffy Miter Clamp

Starting with four regular spring-type clamps, I made a set of these miter clamps in about 30 minutes. You can return the clamp to its original purpose by removing the screws and restoring the plastic tips. They do leave small punctures in the wood, but these are easily filled.

Remove plastic tips and drill holes for 1/4-in. x 20 hardened steel bolts.

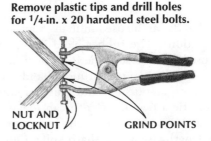

NUT AND LOCKNUT   **GRIND POINTS**

Jeff Hoffa
Renwick, WV

Quick'N Easy Spring Clamps

Saw 2- or 3-in. dia. PVC pipe into rings an inch or so wide and saw them open. They'll provide about eight pounds of pressure when opened about an inch. They may not be as convenient as one-handed spring clamps, but since you'll get more than a hundred of them from a 10-ft. length of PVC pipe, at least the price is right.

Tom Whalen
Cohoes, NY

Spreading Contact Cement

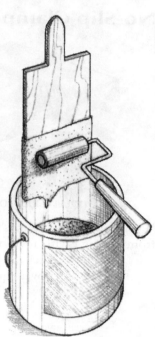

Contact cement is easy to apply with a roller, but it's hard to clean solvent based contact cement from a paint tray. To avoid this mess, make a paddle from a piece of 1/4-in. plywood, narrow enough to fit into the cement can. Dip the paddle in the can, pick up some cement, and roll the cement onto your job. Not only is cleanup easier, but you reduce the level of toxic and flammable fumes from an open tray of contact cement. I wear rubber gloves and a respirator with an organic-vapor cartridge (available from Direct Safety Co., 7815 South 46th St., Phoenix, AZ 85044).

Rod Goettelmann
Southampton Township, NJ

Rubber Band Clamps

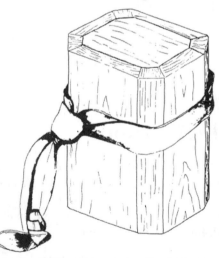

Large rubber bands can be used in many ways in gluing and assembly operations. The rubber band clamps that I have found most useful are those made from bicycle inner tubes. One inner tube will make two or more bands. Try to make the bands as long as possible and when smaller ones are needed, simply tie a new knot. You can make these bands by cutting out the valve stems of the inner tube and splitting the tube lengthwise with a sharp knife. Old inner tubes should be available at a bicycle shop.

Frank Pittman

A Glue Pot Idea

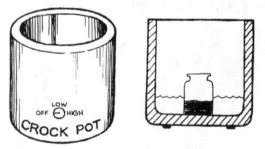

Hot animal glue is still preferred for a number of woodworking operations. One of the problems with this adhesive is the fact that it requires a glue pot. Commercially made glue pots are wonderful tools but usually cost from about $60.00 up. I've had good luck for several years using an electric "garden variety" crock pot to heat glue. You can find crock pots on sale sometimes for about $15.00. I use the pot like a double boiler, putting the glue in a small glass jar and placing it in water which is in the pot. I have also heard that some people have good luck using electric baby bottle warmers for the same purpose.

Frank Pittman

Painless Squeeze-Out Removal

I've come up with a method to remove hardened glue lines. Attach two strips of Plexiglas or 1/4-in. plywood to the base of a router with double-stick tape. Chuck a 1/2-in. wide straight bit into the router and set the depth so the bit barely grazes the surface of the stock. Run the router along the glue line and you're in business.

Ben Erickson
Eutaw, AL

Clamping Wood Edging

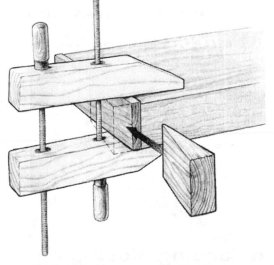

If you want to install edging on a shelf or counter and don't have any edging clamps, try small, wood hand screws, instead. Apply the edging strips, and then position the clamps, leaving a gap of about 1/2 in. between the screw and the edging strip. Tap wedges into the gap until you see glue squeezing out. If the edging is slightly wider than the countertop, toe in the clamp slightly.

Dave Sellers
Emmaus, PA

Old-Fashioned Glue Spreader

This is a quick, easy way to spread glue when using biscuit joiners. Grind an old putty knife to the profile of a standard biscuit, squirt the slot with glue and spread it with the blade. Wipe the steel off immediately and you'll have no cleanup problem.

Thomas Wilson
San Diego, CA

Grind tip to profile of biscuit.

Disposable Spreader

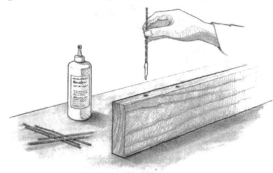

Pipe cleaners are excellent for spreading glue in dowel holes or biscuit-joint slots. I also use them for applying stains and finishes in hard-to-reach spots.

Ralph Meyer
Nashotah, WI

Sanding and Scraping

Sander Savvy

A sheet of fine sandpaper (220-grit and finer) doesn't last too long when you're sanding with an electric sander.

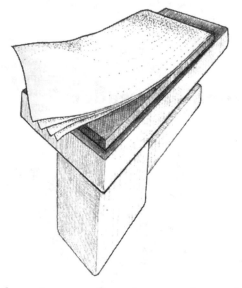

Instead of stopping every five minutes to change the paper, put on four or five sheets at one time. When the top sheet wears out or tears, just rip it off to expose the next sheet.

Herbert Zohner
Petalurna, CA

Sandpaper Cutter

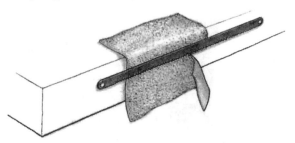

To tear sandpaper to size, loosely tack or screw a hacksaw blade to the edge of your workbench, teeth down. Slip the paper behind the hacksaw blade with the desired amount below the teeth and tear it toward you.

Brian A. Green
Foam Lake, SK, Canada

Folding Sandpaper

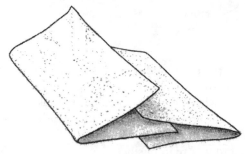

When sanding by hand, I use two quarter sheets of sandpaper folded in half and interlocked. I can then flip the paper over for a finer or coarser grit. When the sandpaper gets worn, I reverse the interlock. I also find that sandpaper folded this way stays in my hand better than a single piece folded in half.

David Hurd
Madison, WI

Folding Sandpaper—Again

Here's another way to fold sandpaper that a local boat-builder showed me. You cut the sandpaper halfway through and then fold it as shown. It makes a nice, thick pad and nowhere is the grit rubbing against itself.

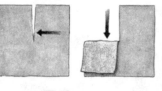

Madeleine Johnson
Halifax, Nova Scotia

Hand-Sanding Blocks

I make my own sanding blocks by gluing sheet cork (spray adhesive works best) to $3/4$-in. birch plywood. This gives me a hard surface on one side and a soft one on the other. After cutting the plywood into pieces of a convenient size, I soften the edges with sandpaper. Cut them into smaller blocks and they make handy clamping pads.

K. Kelzer
Freeland, WA

Filing Sandpaper

This sandpaper holder keeps the paper flat and organized by grit—and you can readily check your supply. The base is 3/4-in. plywood; I made the dividers from 1/4-in. plywood. A lead weight, placed on top, keeps everything flat.

Tim Green
Lancaster, CA

Full-Sheet Sanding Pad

I don't like to waste time cutting up sandpaper to fit a sanding block, so I made this custom block to fit the paper instead. Just cut a piece of 3/4-in. plywood to the proper, width, and  saw a groove along one edge with the tablesaw. To get the paper started, slip one edge into the groove, wrap the paper around the block as shown, and slip the other end of the paper into the groove. Then you can slide the paper down the block. To hold lightweight paper in place, slide a tongue depressor into the slot to take up slop.

Bruce Hogan
Long Branch, NJ

Parking a Sander

When using an orbital finishing sander, I find it helpful to have a 12-in. sq. piece of carpet close by. The power can be turned off and the sander safely set on the carpet before it has come to a complete stop.

John Hisey
Bainbridge Island, WA

Sanding Flat

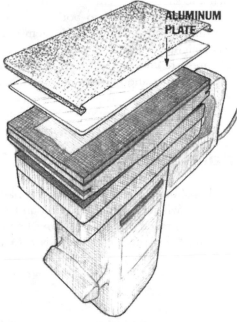

ALUMINUM PLATE

When sanding a large, flat surface with an electric pad sander, excessive pressure can result in a wavy surface because the soft rubber pad allows the sandpaper to dip down into softer areas and remove more material. To eliminate this problem, install a 1/16-in. thick aluminum plate between the rubber pad and the sandpaper when a flat surface is important. Make sure that the aluminum plate is flat and its edges and corners are smooth and generously rounded to prevent it from marring the work if it accidentally touches it. Fasten the plate to the rubber pad with double-sided carpet tape.

Walter J. Morrison
Northport, NY

Flat Sanding Surface

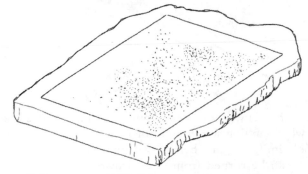

A small flat scrap of Warble or granite can be converted into an excellent foundation surface for sanding small parts. Small slabs 3/4-in. to 1-in. thick are usually heavy enough to be used on a bench top without a hold down. Be sure to check the surface of the slab for flatness before using it. The one I am now using was made from a piece of an old broken marble table top. After you have found a slab, simply tape a sheet of abrasive paper to the surface and sand.

Frank Pittman

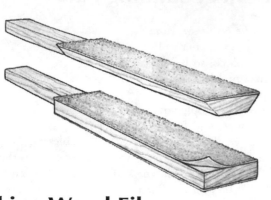

Making Wood Files

I have been making sandpaper and scrap-wood "wood files" for years and find them useful for such things as sanding right up to an inside corner. For extremely tight places, you can bevel one or both edges at 45 degrees. To make the files, I rip scrap wood into strips about 3/8 in. thick, 1 1/2 in. to 2 in. wide, and the length of the abrasive paper I want to use. (If you want a handle, leave some extra length.)

To attach the sandpaper, cut pieces the same width as the wood strips and glue them to both sides of the wood, using a thin film of yellow glue. I stack them up, five or six high and lay weights on top of the pile until the glue cures. (Too much pressure and you'll force the glue through the paper.) Silicon-carbide and aluminum oxide abrasive sandpaper work well.

Ronald J. Hughes

Bump-Free Curves

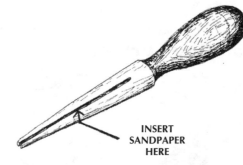

To sand curves bump free, try this: save the waste material and cut it into small pieces (about 8 or 9-in. long), staple sandpaper along the cut edge and sand. Any irregularities produced by band sawing will be worn down. For a circular piece, one section will work all the way around. For free form curves, each section of waste is used for the corresponding section of curve.

Christian Becksvoort

A Padded Round Sanding Block

A guitar maker showed me this idea, and it has proven to be very valuable when sanding contours and curved surfaces. The block is made from a 1-in. dowel approximately 6-in. long. The foam rubber padding is actually a fairly

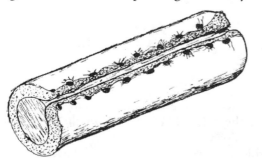

dense foam used in making knee and elbow pads for athletes. This material is sold in roll form and is sometimes hard to obtain in small pieces. You might contact a football or basketball coach or a sporting goods shop to obtain a small piece. The foam is wrapped in place. This soft round block can make many otherwise tough around the dowel and tacked or glued sanding jobs easier.

Frank Pittman

A Tapered Round Sanding Block

INSERT
SANDPAPER
HERE

There are many times when a round sanding block is essential when sanding scrolls and other small curves. I first saw a tool similar to this being used by a violin maker. The block can be turned from any hardwood. The one I use most is made from hard maple. The size of the tapered section can vary. Mine has a 5-in. long taper which is 1-in. diameter at the large end and 3/16-in. at the small end. The handle is approximately 3 1/2-in. long and turned to feel good in your hand. A saw kerf is made approximately 4 1/2-in. down the taper on a band saw. Use a V-block when doing this job. To use the block, simply insert a corner of a piece of sandpaper into the kerf and wrap it around.

Frank Pittman

Coping Sander

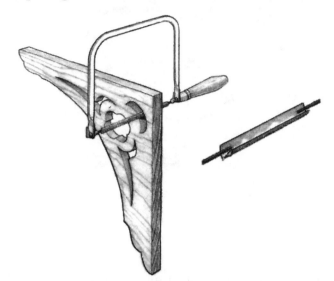

To sand small, inside holes on a project, I glue the broken end of a coping saw blade to a strip of cloth-backed abrasive. When the glue dries, I insert the strip through the project and mount it in the coping saw.

John Teehee
Hilo, HI

Deluxe Sanding Block

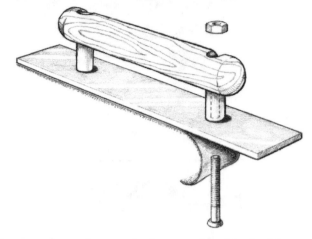

These are far and away the best sanding blocks I have ever used. I make each one 6-in. to 36-in. long and 2-in. wide for the carborundrum cloth I use. This comes in rolls so you can just cut off what you need. I attach the abrasive with spray adhesive or glue stick.

Jay Wallace
Ashland, OR

Sanding Saws

These easy-to-make tools have almost replaced rasps and wood files in my shop. I bandsaw the handle out of $3/4$-in. plywood, then tack a strip of cloth-backed sanding belt at each end. I keep different frames for each of the grits I commonly use. These sanding saws are especially useful on convex surfaces or when finishing a lathe turning.

Vary the dimensions of the frame and the tension in the strip and you get different degrees of contact with the work.

Karl Schuman
New York, NY

Contoured Sanding Blocks

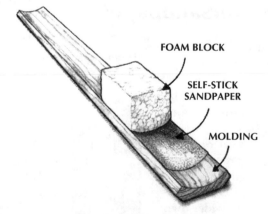

FOAM BLOCK

SELF-STICK
SANDPAPER

MOLDING

If a lot of molding needs to be sanded, apply 80-grit self-stick sandpaper neatly and carefully to several inches of the molding. Then rub a block of foam insulation on the abrasive molding until the foam block matches all of the contours of the molding. Finally, remove the self-stick paper from the molding, apply an appropriate grit to the foam block, and sand the molding.

Trebor Narom
Onaled, MN

Changing Sander Belts

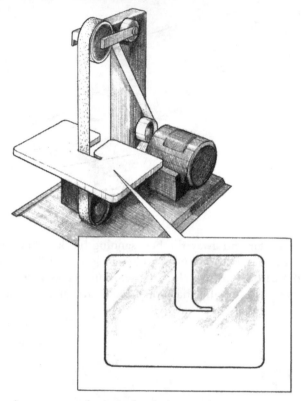

To change a sander/grinder belt you have to remove the table on most machines. To change belts without removing the table, cut a slot with a sweep to one side as shown. This allows you to remove the belt easily.

Bill Brown
Redford, MI

Slip-On Sandpaper

I found an easy way to slip sandpaper onto a sleeveless drum sander. First, get a dowel the same diameter and length as the drum sander. Bevel one end and cut a groove in the dowel lengthwise.

Cut a piece of sandpaper 1/2 in. wider than the length of the dowel and long enough to fit around the dowel and into the groove. Slip the sandpaper over the dowel with 1/2 in. protruding past the beveled end. Slide the sandpaper down over the drum. A little baby powder on the drum helps slip the sandpaper on easier.

Tony Kosykoski
Belle Vernon, PA

Dust-Free Sanding

For dust-free drum sanding on your drill press, build a sanding table to clamp to your drill-press table as shown in the drawing. The 3/8-in. thick Lexan inserts allow you to use different-diameter drums and maintain a 1/8 in. maximum clearance between the drum and the insert.

Jeff Chancey
Stevensville, MI

Stop Score Marks

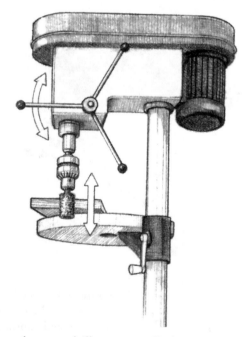

A drum sander on a drill press usually leaves score marks on the workpiece. You can prevent the scoring by moving the drum up and down during the final sanding. The combined vertical and circular motion is similar to the action of an expensive oscillating spindle sander.

Stephen Blaisdell
Naugatuck, CT

Lathe Sanding Drum

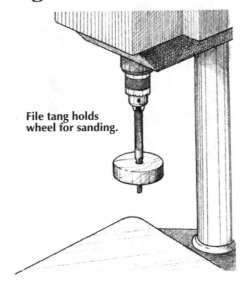

You can make your own sanding drum for your lathe. Turn two wooden plugs with a shoulder on the edge, sized to fit standard sanding-drum sleeves as shown in the drawing. Slip a sleeve on one plug, jam the sleeve full of sawdust and/or shavings, fit the second plug, and hold it all together between the head-stock and tail-stock. Turn on the lathe and go to it. You can adjust the firmness of the drum by how tightly you jam in the sawdust and shavings.

Lyle Terrell
New Orleans, LA

Sanding Wooden wheels

File tang holds wheel for sanding.

I cut wooden toy wheels with an adjustable-circle cutter that leaves a 1/4 in. hole in the center and a "tread" that requires sanding. I cut the end off a 3/8-in. rat-tail file (the file must be heated with a propane torch first to remove the temper) and chuck the handle end of the file in the drill press with the tang pointing down. I press a wheel onto the tang, which provides enough of a grip to hold the wheel for sanding. Run the drill press at a relatively low speed (300 to 400 RPM).

Richard Wnuk
Kalamazoo, MI

Belt Sander Tracking

MASKING TAPE

If the belt on your belt sander won't track properly no matter how you adjust it, place two or three wraps of masking tape around the center of one of the drums. This usually fixes the problem.

Ron Oakes
Brea, CA

Hand-friendly Scraper

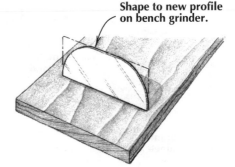

Shape to new profile on bench grinder.

Scraper blades are usually steel rectangles with sharp corners—all four of them. Finding this hard on my hands, I grind the blade to the more comfortable profile illustrated. Incidentally, the steel in panel saws makes excellent scrapers. Take a worn-out saw to a sheet metal shop and they'll cut any size scraper blanks you want.

John Grew-Sheridan
San Francisco, CA

Rounding Ends of Turnings

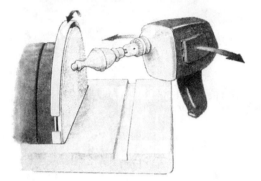

The quickest and easiest way for me to round the end of a finial after turning it between centers is to chuck it in a drill and sand it round on my disc sander with the drill running.

David Johnson
Apple Valley MN

New Angle on Belt Sanding

To remove a large amount of waste wood quickly with a belt sander, turn the sander to a 45 degree angle with the grain. Sand until you're near the level desired and then gradually change the angle so the final sanding is done with the grain of the wood.

David Johnson
Apple Valley, MN

Simple Circle-Sander

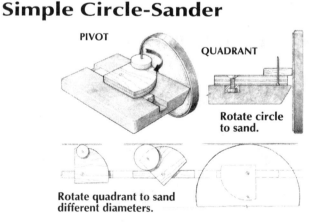

PIVOT

QUADRANT

Rotate circle
to sand.

Rotate quadrant to sand
different diameters.

I made this simple jig for sanding the edges of rounds, the wheels of wooden toys, etc. By rotating the quadrant about its pivot point you can sand discs from 1 1/2 in. up to 11 in. The quadrant is screwed to a short piece of 3/4-in. stock that fits the slot on a conventional disc sander. As an alternative, you could rig it up to work with a belt sander.

Jay Wallace
Ashland, OR

Spin-Polish

You can sand (wire-brush, buff) small round objects like knobs by mounting them on a slightly loose fitting dowel or rod and letting the tool spin them as it does its sanding. Adjust the angle between the rod and the tool to get the amount of spin and abrasion that you want. A piece of tubing over the rod will help to keep the knob from running off the end.

Russell Field
Federal Way, WA

Sanding Small Pieces

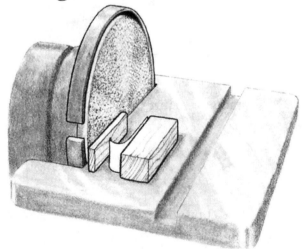

When sanding thin stock on a disc sander, you can easily trim your fingernails along with the wood if you aren't careful. I keep my fingers clear by using double-stick tape to attach the stock to a larger block. This works equally well with a belt sander.

H.R. McDermid
Vernon, B.C., Canada

After the Fruitcake

Don't throw that cake tin out! Cut in half and mounted on the wall, it makes an ideal holder for sanding discs. I color-code the tins—red and blue—so I know which holds the fine disks and which the coarse.

Howard Moody
Upper Jay, NY

No-clog Files

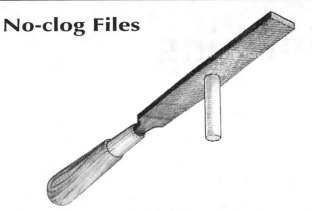

Soft, non-ferrous metals like brass and aluminum will clog a file pretty quickly. Rub your file with a piece of chalk and you'll find the file teeth won't clog nearly as fast.

Lazlo Spectrum
Tucson, AZ

Cutting Sandpaper to Size

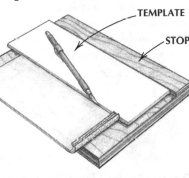

TEMPLATE

STOP

I use this handy jig to cut full sheets of sandpaper in half, quarters—whatever I need. I position multiple sheets against the stop, abrasive side down, and place a template on top that's the same size as the sheet I want. Then I cut the stack of sheets with a razor or mat knife. I used Dupont Corian for the template, but plywood, particleboard or hardboard, edged with plastic, would do the job.

Phil Brooks
Medford, NJ

Sanding Tip

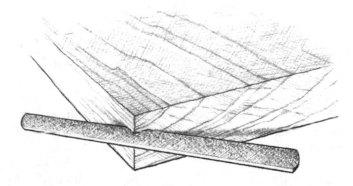

An ordinary emery board can handle a lot of fine sanding jobs, particularly on thin stock. There's a coarse and a fine side and, for tight spots, you can cut one end to a point with a pair of scissors.

R.J. Rhodes
Lincoln, NE

Update Your Sander

If the pad on your orbital sander wasn't made for adhesive-backed sandpaper, stick duct tape edge to edge over the pad and around the edges. The sandpaper will adhere to the duct tape and will peel from the tape without tearing up the pad.

Walter J. Martin
Buffalo, NY

Finishing

Painting Stilts

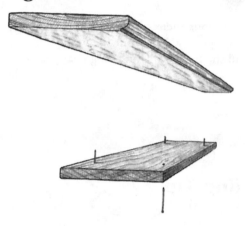

Plaques and other flat pieces need a finish on every side to prevent cupping. Painting stilts let you finish all sides at once. To make the stilts, sharpen three or four six-penny finish nails, and drive them all the way through a piece of $3/8$-in. plywood. To use the stilts, finish the bottom of the piece first, then lay it bottom down on the stilts to finish the top and edges. Styrofoam stuck on the nail points will protect you from the pointed stilts when not in use.

David Black
Barnwell, SC

No-Scratch Surfaces for Finish Work

When a project reaches the finishing stage, I protect my work surfaces from finishing materials and the project from scratches by covering the work surfaces with carpet. Because I put large projects on sawhorses for finishing, I made up carpeted, fitted forms for the sawhorses. I store the forms, carpeted-side down, to keep them dust free.

H. Wesley Phillips
Greer SC

Turning the Tables

Here's a good way to support a panel or door while finishing. Put one nail in one end of the panel and two nails in the other end so it can't rock. When you've applied finish to one side, turn the panel over by lifting the end with the two nails and pivoting the panel on the single nail on the other end. Once your finish is in place, leave the panel on the sawhorse to dry.

Carl Dorsch
Pittsburgh, PA

Punching Copper

I recently made a pie safe for my wife, and of course she wanted the doors decorated with punched copper panels in traditional fashion. Punching four large panels, all by hand, was going to take time, so I used my drill press. I took the handle off an ice pick, chucked the steel needle in the drill chuck and set the copper sheet, backed with plywood, on the table underneath. By setting the drill press depth stop I could get a consistent hole in the copper sheet every time. With the drill running, it was easy to withdraw the ice pick.

John Eiler
Riverdale, GA

Precise Door Alignment

Mounting hinges on small doors or lids to the proper clearance or alignment can be a frustrating problem. When I use a hinge that requires a mortise on the case but not on the door or lid, I first cut the mortise and screw the hinge to the case. Next, I close the hinge, put a drop of hot-melt glue on the unattached leaf and lay the door in place carefully aligned. When the glue sets in a minute or two I add the screws.

David Johnson
Apple Valley, MN

Smoothing Edges on Acrylics

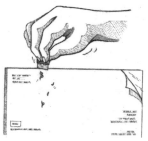

Even a sharp carbide-tipped blade will leave saw marks when cutting acrylics. Here's a quick way to get them out. Take a single-edge razor blade, skewed slightly to the direction of travel, and scrape the edge. Then gently chamfer the corners. Strip off the protective paper and make a light pass with a propane torch. This will remove any remaining marks and leave a polished edge.

Alex Moll
Marysville, WA

Flame-Polish

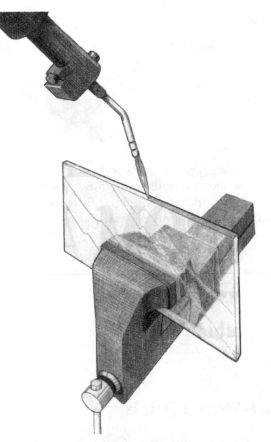

For a professional looking edge treatment on Plexiglas, try "flame-polishing." First sand out saw marks, then lick the edges lightly with a propane torch. The scratches disappear and the edge takes on a glossy finish. Practice on scrap to get a feel for the process.

David Bloch
Barnwell, SC

No Sweat Brass Polishing

Before installing brass hardware on any of my projects I first toss it into a vibrating case polisher to clean it. These devices are intended for cleaning ammunition cartridges before reloading and consist of a container of fine talcum powder attached to an electric motor. It's the vibration produced by this motor that does the cleaning and polishing. The machine is very effective for cleaning nooks and crannies that are impossible to reach with a brush or rag. Even better, there are no caustic chemicals involved, nothing to wipe off, and no elbow grease. I bought mine at a sporting goods store where you'll find several versions.

Michael Chilquist
Pittsburgh, PA

Cure for Hard Putty Sticks

Colored putty sticks are handy for filling nail holes, but they sometimes get hard with age and become difficult to use.

When this happens, I soften the stick before using it by immersing the end in very hot water for about a minute. Don't put too much of the stick in the water, or the stick will get too soft to hold properly.

Walter Morrison
Northport, NY

Filling Dents

To fill a depression in wood, first drill shallow holes in the depression at slightly different angles. This helps to anchor the filling. Overfill the area just a bit and allow to harden, then sand flush.

Frank Pittman

Removing Dents

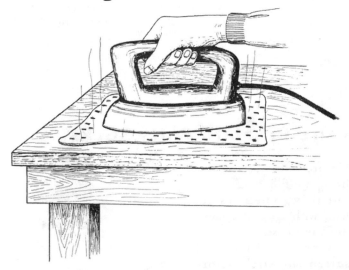

Here is an old, but effective, tip. To get dents out of wood, first wet a cloth. Hold the wet cloth on the dent and surrounding wood and press with a hot iron. As long as the cloth is moist, there is no danger of scorching the wood.

Tim Harlow
Macon, MS

Sticky Fingers

To get the surface clean at the final finishing stages of a project, I wrap a couple inches of masking tape (sticky-side out) around my left forefinger, and if I spot a speck of sawdust or other foreign matter, I pick it up with the tape.

Lane Olinghouse
Everett, WA

Magnetic Fuzz Buster

After rubbing down a finish with steel wool, I want to get rid of the metal strands left behind. To do this, I take a magnetic screwdriver bit holder, fit it with a bit that will get in the crevices of my project, and pick up the small particles of steel wool with it.

John Hisey
Bainbridge Island, WA

Hot-Wax Finish

When I was growing up in China, I used to make carving knives with wooden handles. I couldn't get varnish, shellac or other types of finish, so I dipped the bare wood in paraffin (candle wax) heated on the stove. The result was a very durable and waterproof finish—I still use it from time to time.

Yeung Chan
Millbrae, CA

Keeping Finishes Fresh

Here's a way to save paints and finishes in a can. Just pour a thin layer of the appropriate thinner on top of the material and cover. Put the can on the shelf without shaking. When you want to use it, stir in the thinner and the finish is good as new.

Frank Distefano
Rochester, NY

Be Kind to Your Nozzles

I use a variety of spray finishes and adhesives in my business, and I can't afford clogged and splattered finishes. So, I have devised this simple solution: I save the small, plastic nozzle cap that comes with each can and pour in just enough paint thinner to cover the nozzle. when I am through spraying, I don't need to clear the nozzle but just invert it and push it down onto its cap. The can stays there, upside down, until the next time I need it.

Norm Fried
Oceanside, CA

Preserving Tung Oil

The same chemistry that allows polymerized tung oil products to harden to such a fine finish on the wood also allows larger quantities of the stuff to gel and become unusuable if exposed to air even the small amount of air left in an only partly used container. The best way to solve this problem is simply to top up the container with water every time you use a bit of the oil. The water sinks to the bottom, the tung oil product floats discreetly on top. The two liquids do not otherwise affect each other. You can do this topping up in the original tin container, or after the first opening you can transfer the oil to a large wide-mouth glass jar (pickle jar, peanut butter jar, quart canning jar), which lets you dip your rag, sponge, brush, fingers, or whatever directly into the top of the container.

Mark H. Robbins
Milford, PA

No-Dirt Dip

To avoid getting dust or dirt into varnish and other finishes, don't dip the brush directly into the can. Use a disposable plastic cup to dip out a portion of the finish from the can. This leaves the remaining finish clean and, since you aren't pouring out of the can, the rim stays clean for a tight closure.

Bob Lipscomb
Concord, GA

Freezing Brushes

What do you do with a brush covered with oil-based paints or varnish that you'll need again in a day or two? Rinse it out in earth-polluting petrochemicals? No, there's a better way: Just put the brush in a Zip-Loc bag and stick it in the freezer. when needed again let it thaw (still in the bag) at room temperature. This works for foam, bristle or nylon brushes. If your spouse is concerned about smelling up the refrigerator, use two bags, one inside the other. To reuse a bag, turn it inside out and let the paint dry.

Robert Schneider
Los Angeles, CA

Recycled Brush Cleaner

When using alkyd (oil-based) paints, I clean the brushes by rinsing them in kerosene. I keep the solvent in glass Mason jars which come with screw-on lids and rubber seals. I let the sediment settle to the bottom and then pour off the clear solvent into another jar and use it again. Kerosene evaporates slowly and so very little gets released into the atmosphere. The glass jars eventually go to their reward at the recycling center.

Laura Sanchez
San Francisco CA

Furniture Making With Finesse

Edge Banding Made Easy

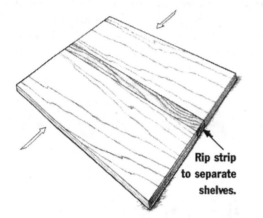

Rip strip to separate shelves.

When facing plywood shelves with solid stock, do two shelves at once. Glue a 1⁵/₈-in. wide strip of wood between two plywood shelves. When dry, rip the strip down the middle. You'll have a ³/₄-in. solid facing on each shelf with a perfect joint in less time with fewer clamps.

Brian J. O'Connor
Wolverine, MI

Trimming Wood Edging

Solid-wood strips are often glued to the edges of plywood shelves or tabletops. But planing them flush with the plywood can be a problem. If you plane too deeply, you'll cut through the face veneer on the plywood. To avoid this, I draw several short pencil lines across the glue joint, as shown. I watch these lines and stop planing immediately when they disappear.

James Schenfield
Dayton, OH

Not for Turning Knobs

Wooden knobs—the kind with a single screw—often become loose and twist in the hand. To cure this, I drill a pilot hole in the back of the knob and insert a small brad or nail with the point protruding ¹/₈ in. or so When this nail bites into the drawer front, the knob will never turn again. If your bits aren't small enough to drill the pilot hole, cut the head off the nail or brad and use it as a drill.

Robert Campbell
Somerset, PA

Gluing Up Polygons

When trying to make a many-sided project, whether flat like a picture frame or coopered like an architectural column, tiny angle errors accumulate and become a big error when all of the parts are brought together. Instead of fiddling endlessly with impossibly fine adjustments of each angle, I glue up the parts in two halves. I then plane the joining surfaces flat before gluing the two halves together to make the whole.

Glenn Hughes
Dublin, PA

Foolproof Board Joining

The first step when joining a number of boards for a table-top is to run the edges over a jointer so they're flat and square. Before doing so I always check that the jointer fence is dead square to the table. But even so, the edges sometimes end up a fraction off, leaving gaps in my joints. I recently discovered I can compensate for slight errors in the fence setting by alternating the boards as I feed them through the machine. I send the first board through with the good face against the fence, the next with the good face away from the fence. In this way any small errors cancel each other out instead of adding up.

Judy Anderson
Ann Arbor, MI

Slotting the Aprons

I like to attach my tabletops to the aprons with metal tabletop fasteners, or buttons, to allow for seasonal movement.

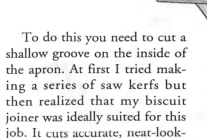

To do this you need to cut a shallow groove on the inside of the apron. At first I tried making a series of saw kerfs but then realized that my biscuit joiner was ideally suited for this job. It cuts accurate, neat-looking slots, and the #0 setting gives you the right depth. If the legs interfere with the location of the slots, cut the slot before gluing up the base.

George Pease
Fortuna, CA

Vacuum Bagging On the Cheap

No need to blow your bait and beer money on a $400 vacuum pump. For small projects—veneering jewelry boxes, for example—I use a Ziploc freezer bag attached to a hand-operated vacuum pump. These simple pumps, (Mityvac is one brand) are made to bleed brake systems; cost around $30 and are available in most automotive parts stores. To make a leak-proof seal where the tube enters the bag, snip one corner off, insert the tube and lay a piece of duct tape underneath it, sticky side up. Put another piece on top and firmly flatten everything out.

Michael Chilquist
Pittsburgh, PA

Turning the Leg Out

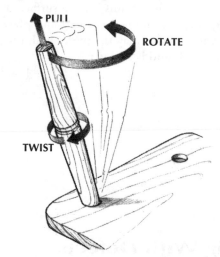

Repairing chairs usually involves some disassembly—pulling rungs out of legs and extracting legs from the wooden seat. My method is to clamp the seat in a vise, or, if the back is off, put it on the floor and kneel on it. Then I grasp the recalcitrant leg with both hands and simultaneously twist it counterclockwise while rotating it clockwise. At the same time I pull. Even wedged legs can be coaxed out in this way.

Jason Richardson
Binghamton, NY

Making Multiple Inlay Items

Inlay work frequently requires the use of items of identical size and shape. for example, a Hepplewhite bell flower pattern will require several matching veneer flowers. I produce these by first preparing a "veneer sandwich". Simply select several pieces of veneer suitable for the design and glue them together with one sheet of craft paper between each ply. If four identical patterns are needed glue up at least five or six plies to be sure of a yield of four good pieces. After this veneer assembly has dried, at least overnight, lay out the desired shapes on the surface of the sandwich.

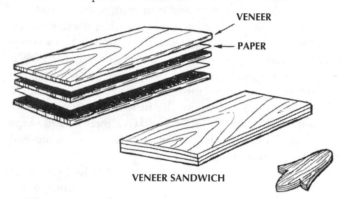

VENEER

PAPER

VENEER SANDWICH

The items can be cut out with a precision scroll saw or a hand coping or jeweler's saw. The edges of the designs can be filed, sanded and smoothed while they are still glued together. After all shaping is complete, the individual pieces can be split from the sandwich by carefully placing a knife edge on the paper joint and slicing off sections, one at a time. The paper which remains on the surface of the inlay items actually helps strengthen the part and prevents splintering of delicate points. Inlay the pieces with the paper still on the surfaces and sand it off later.

Frank Pittman

A Diamond Match In Veneers

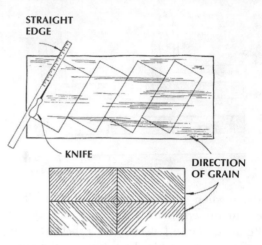

STRAIGHT EDGE

KNIFE

DIRECTION OF GRAIN

To create a diamond matched pattern out of veneer, determine the finished overall sizes you need. Secure a single piece of veneer so you can layout the four smaller pieces according to the sketch. Be very careful in preparing the joints. Use veneer tape, which is a specially prepared tape made of very thin paper with lots of glue on it. The taped surface should be up after the pattern has been glued to its base material. This prevents a raised area and allows you to sand off the tape after everything is dry.

Jerry Lyons

Dealing With Defects

How to get the most out of your lumber when sapwood, knots and other defects mar the surface? I make templates for the parts of my furniture out of 1/8-in. hardboard. Then I can lay out the parts on the lumber by tracing around the templates, missing the defects and so minimizing waste. I keep the templates in case I want to make the same piece of furniture again.

W. Curtis Johnson
Corwallis, OR

Fast Steamer

When steaming small pieces of wood for models, I just stick a piece of PVC pipe, 10 or 15 in. long, into the spout of an electric kettle. You have steam, and plenty of it, in minutes. Tie a length of string to the end of the stock so you don't burn your fingers getting it out. Also, be careful not to let the water level get too low or you'll fry the heating element.

Guy Bush
Nova Scotia, Canada

Bump Extractor

Anyone working with laminates knows how annoying it is to discover a lump under the surface. I use an old hacksaw blade as a "bump extractor." Here's how it works: I smooth out the hacksaw teeth on a grinder and then grind a hook at one end of the blade as shown. If a lump shows up, I heat the end of the blade with torch, slip it in between the laminate and the substrate, and grab the alien particle. It works every time.

Brian Gillespie
Newfoundland, NJ

Barbecue Steamer

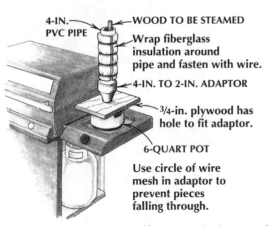

Insulation makes this steamer effective and cheap to build. The heat source is the propane-fired auxiliary burner on my barbecue. I can add water from above, but a 6-quart container is good for at least an hour's steaming. A word of caution: Don't use your spouse's favorite pot—a black, tarry residue appears after a few hours of use.

Dale Chapman
Salt Lake City, UT

Blinds Separate Laminates

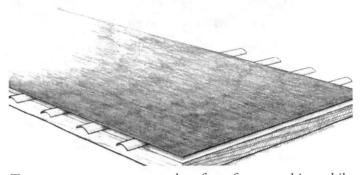

To prevent contact-cemented surfaces from touching while I position plastic laminate on the underlay stock, I place individual strips of old venetian blinds between them. They pull out easily, dropping the laminate onto the surface.

J. A. Wilson
Lexington, MA

Creating Veneer Joints

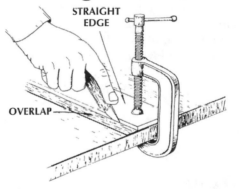

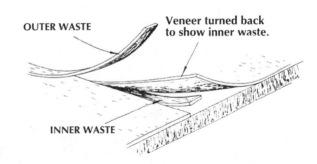

Use a super sharp X-acto knife in conjunction with a straight edge to cut the veneer straight. The species of veneer, however, will dictate whether you might want to moisten the veneer a little with a sponge. Cap the two pieces over each other and make the cut through both pieces at the same time. Remove excess and prepare for gluing.

Jen Chiles

Arm Chair Joint

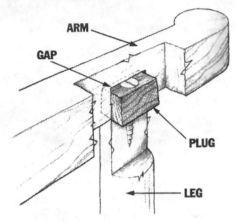

Here's a joint that I think is an improvement over mortise-and-tenons or dowels for joining chair arms to legs. Mortise and tenon joints or dowel joints glue the long fibers of the tenon or dowel across the grain of the arm. Seasonal wood movement can eventually break the glue bond and weaken these joints after a few years.

My joint uses a wood screw to fasten a wooden plug to the leg. The plug glues into a recess in the arm. You align the grain of the plug with the grain of the arm for a strong glue joint. If you're worrying about the holding power of the screw in end grain, don't. The force required to pull out a #10 woodscrew with $1^1/2$ in. of thread engaged in hardwood end grain ranges from a low of 298 lbs. in poplar to 1236 lbs. in maple.

Michael O'Banion
Westminster, MD

No-Rout Screw Slots

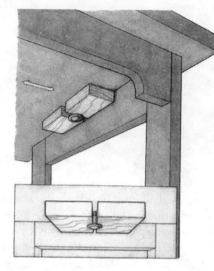

Here's an easy way to attach tabletops or cabinet tops. Like the screw-in-slotted-hole method, it allows the top to move but doesn't require any routing to produce the slot. The screw slot is formed by the gap between two $3/4$ by $1^1/2$ by 2-in. wooden blocks glued to the under-structure of the top. Use the intended screw as a spacer to separate the blocks. When the screw is installed, it can slide between the blocks as the top expands and contracts.

Pat Warner
Escondido, CA

Plug Puller

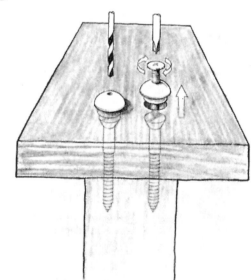

Here's a sure-fire way to remove a button plug or a flush plug that covers a screw head. Drill a $1/8$-in. pilot hole through the center of the plug. Then, drive a drywall screw through the center. The hardened drywall screw bottoms on the screw head and forces the plug up out of the hole.

Kent A. Johnson
Evansville, IN

Down the Tube

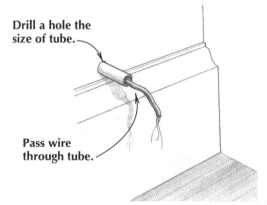

Drill a hole the size of tube.

Pass wire through tube.

To poke a small wire through a hollow wall or cabinet space, first insert a small-diameter piece of conduit, PVC pipe or copper tube. This will guide the wire, which may be too limp to make the journey unaided. Be sure to remove the tube before connecting the wires.

Terry Wells
Ashland, OR

Flush Mount Hanger

This flush-mount "keyhole" hanger allows a plaque, clock, or other project to hang flat against the wall on a screw or nail. In the back of my project, I drill a hole 1/8 in. deep with a 1 in. Forstner bit. Then, on the same center point, I drill a hole 3/8 in. deep with a 7/8 in. Forstner bit. This forms a 1/16-in. shoulder for a disk with a keyhole cutout.

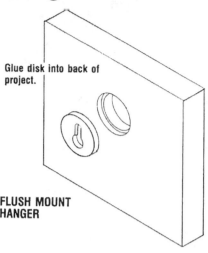

Glue disk into back of project.

FLUSH MOUNT HANGER

I make the 1 in. dia. disk from 1/8-in. thick mahogany plywood. Before cutting out the disk, I form the keyhole by drilling a 5/16 in. dia. hole and a 3/16 in. dia. hole and cutting out between the holes with a sharp chisel. Then I cut out the disk with a scroll saw (a punch would be faster) and glue the disk in place.

J.P. Reichling
Oswego, IL

Installing Cabinets

This device is very useful to hold a top cabinet into place until it can be fastened. It is easy to make and saves a lot of strain when positioning the cabinet. It sits on a base cabinet. To use the cabinet rest, stretch it out and set the top cabinet on it. Then simply push the boards together and the cabinet will rise into position. It is then easily held until a partner fastens the cabinet. Make the sides 18x6-in. Use in pairs.

Tim Harlow
Macon, MS

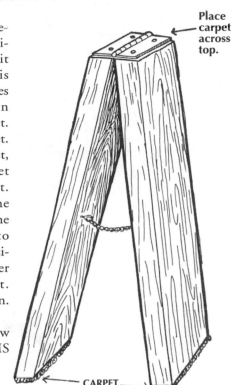

Place carpet across top.

CARPET

Chiseling Out Dovetails

When I clean out corners of half-blind and full-blind dovetails, I find a skew chisel helpful. The angled edge gets into the corners that a straight chisel can't.

Gerald R. Randolph
Danbury, WI

American Woodworker's Tech Tips column has been illustrated, since 1988, by Heather Brine Lambert of Avon, CT, and most of the drawings in this volume are by her. The magazine column's editor is Simon Watts, a woodworker, journalist and teacher who lives in San Francisco.

On the cover: Bob Moran tapers a part using a tablesaw jig like the one shown on page 35.

Project manager: John Kelsey
Typesetting and page makeup: Morgan B. Kelsey
Proofreading and clerking: Larry Green
Cover design: Kitty Pierce Mace